NEWBURY
AND
SPEENHAMLAND.

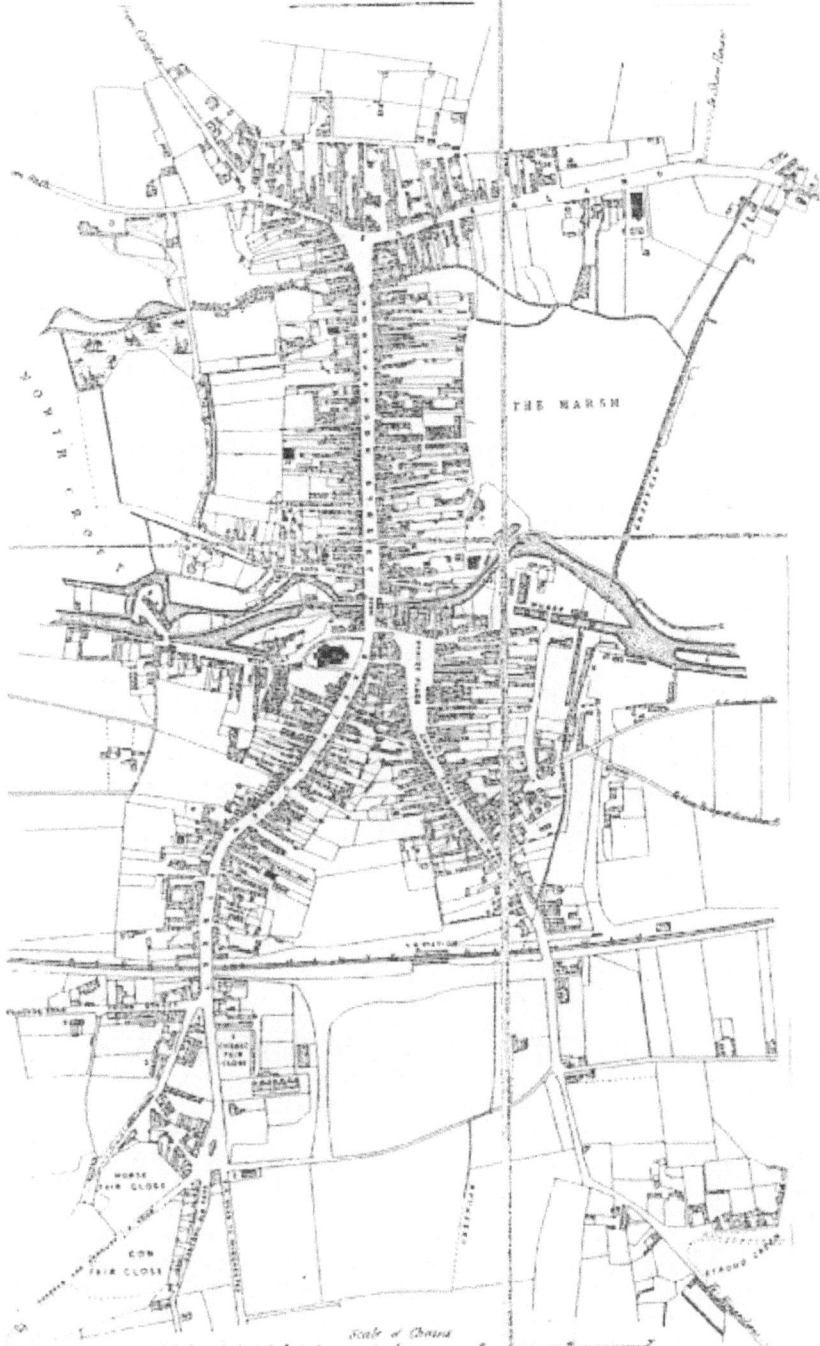

I0134284

THE MARSH

SOKE CROFT

HORSE FAIR CLOSE

COB FAIR CLOSE

Scale of Chains

To Fern

NEWBURY BOROUGH POLICE
1836 - 1875

RICHARD GODFREY

HERESY PUBLISHING

Richard Godfrey The Doghouse, 10 Salcombe Road, Newbury, Berks. RG14. 6ED.

Second Edition 2018

ISBN 978-1-909237-01-8

Published by

Charlie Farrow, Heresy Publishing, Newbury RG14 5JG

ACKNOWLEDGEMENTS

I am truly indebted to many local people and various institutions that have provided material and general information which has proved to be extremely useful in the preparation of this book.

The following people have been particularly helpful:

First and foremost I must thank Sandy Mathieson, who has given up many hours of her own time to edit my original notes, type up various drafts and typeset the final copy. Without her help the whole project would have been far more difficult and time consuming.

I would like to thank the staff in the Berkshire County Record Office at Coley Avenue in Reading especially Sabina Sutherland, who has had to put up with some of my more persistent enquiries which could only be answered by additional research on her part.

This applies equally to both Jane Burrell and Philip Wood of the West Berkshire Museum at Wharf Road in Newbury, who have assisted me greatly with my research by supplying me with much additional information and numerous photographs.

I also thank the staff of Newbury and Reading libraries and the staff at the Newbury Weekly News who have all been extremely helpful to me.

Last but by no means least I would like to thank Mrs. Irene Rodrick for her proof-reading and my good friend Andy Reid, who managed to locate copies of various old documents for me.

Richard Godfrey

MINOR AMENDMENTS TO THE FIRST EDITION

On page 4 of the first publication it was wrongly stated that at the time of formation of the various borough forces under the provision of the Municipal Corporations Act 1835, that the cost of financing the forces was split between both local and central government. In actual fact this provision did not come into effect as far as the central government was concerned, until such time as the County and Borough Police Act 1856, was introduced, which made it mandatory for all counties who had as yet not done so, to form their own police forces.

Since the original publication was printed some additional noteworthy information relating to Sergeant Stillman has come to hand, in so far as in 1871, he was awarded a Testimonial on Vellum by the Royal Humane Society inacknowledgement of his courage and humanity by jumping into the canal in order to save the life of a woman who had attempted suicide.

My thanks to Mrs J. Goddard for bringing this second matter to my attention.

Richard Godfrey 2018

CONTENTS

ACKNOWLEDGEMENTS
MINOR AMENDMENTS
FOREWORD
LIST OF ILLUSTRATIONS
INTRODUCTION

page

CHAPTER I   Historic and legal background   1

CHAPTER 2   Formation of the Force
                Appointment of the first Chief Constable
                and other Officers   9

CHAPTER 3   The First Five Years (1836- 40)
                Jail Breaks
                Dismissal of Night Constable
                Baby's Body in Basket   14

CHAPTER 4   1841 - 45, The Formative Years,
                Riots over th e Enclosure Issue, etc.   26

CHAPTER 5   1846-55, The Early Middle Years
                Death of the First Chief Constable
                Death of Two Jailers
                Riot at the Mansion House during
                Parliamentary Elections   32

CHAPTER 6   The Third Decade (1856 - 65),
                The formation of the Berkshire County Constabulary
                Newbury Superintendent enlarges his area of municipal
                        responsibility
                Appointment of a new Sergeant
                Outbreak of Cattle Plague in the Borough   43
CHAPTER 7   1866 - 70, A Double Murder

The Borough acquires a new fire engine
Pay rise for the Force
Fenian Scare
Enrolment of additional Special Constables
Sergeant's late night drinking habit
Resignation and appointment of a number of sergeants
       in quick succession
Public order incident
Licensing issues   55

CHAPTER 8   The final years
Man sentenced to be detained in the town
Stocks
Death of Superintendent Deane
Appointment of Sergeant Goddard as the new Superintendent
Problems involving Superintendent Goddard
       and the Watch Committee
Dismissal of Superintendent Goddard
Early 'Feelers' in respect of amalgamation with
       the Berkshire Constabulary   81

CHAPTER 9   The final months - November 1874 -March 1875
On-going saga involving Superintendent Goddard
Sergeant Stillman ' Fished out of the Canal'
Amalgamation with the Berkshire Constabulary   96

Appendix i   Report of Watch Committee dated 5th February 1836
outlining the recommended formation
of the new Borough Force   105

Appendix ii   Public Notice issued by the Watch Committee and
signed by the Mayor in forming Borough residents
of the formation of the new Force   108

Appendix iii   Report submitted by the Watch Committee to the
full Borough Council, dated 8th March 1836, relating
to the formation of a 'Committee of Managers'   109

Appendix iv   Report to Home Secretary, dated 31st March 1836
outlining details of the formation of the new Force   113

Appendix v   Plan of the Borough Jail in Cheap Street   115

Appendix vi   Report on the duties required of Police Managers   116

Appendix vii   Extract from the ' Police and Constabulary List'
Dated October 1844   119

Appendix viii   Letter written by the Mayor, William Dredge, to the
editor of the Newbury Herald outlining his actions on
releasing a prisoner following an assault on
Captain Willes   120

Appendix ix   Letter from the Home Secretary dated 31st December
addressed to the Mayor and Watch Committee   121

Appendix x   New roster of beats within the Borough   122

Appendix xi   List of 'Special' constables recruited for the
Finian Scare in 1868   124

Appendix xii   Superintendent Goddard's letter to The Times
Dated 4th June 1874   125

Appendix xiii   Lists of annually appointed 'Special ' constables and
some Fire Brigade personnel   126

Appendix xiv   Report from the Watch Committee to the main Council
relating to the proposed amalgamation with the Berkshire
County Constabulary dated 9th December 1874   128

Appendix xv   Obituary to PC. Beck   130

Appendix xvi   Officers serving in the Borough   132

BIBLIOGRAPHY

INDEX

**All photographs in this book are reproduced by kind permission of the
West Berkshire Museum, The Wharf, Newbury**

FOREWORD

Richard Godfrey's chronicle of Newbury Borough's police force is a fascinating account of how it evolved from the old night watch system to a credible law enforcement' organisation, even by 1875. Well researched and written in an easy style, he gives a detailed background of some of the issues of mid 19th century Newbury and the effects the Industrial Revolution had on the mainly rural population in the area. He relates how the Borough Council formally creates Newbury's first paid and uniformed police force which was accountable to the Council's newly created Watch Committee.

Through his detailed research he has been able to identify many of the early individuals on both sides of the legal system and he occasionally uses the vernacular with such phrases as 'lewd and common women ', but this graphically describes certain aspects of life in those days.

This account of the Newbury Borough Police force is unique which merits its inclusion as a significant and important aspect of Newbury's history.

Adrian Edwards
Mayor of Newbury
1990/91 and 2007/08

ILLUSTRATIONS

Inside front cover Town Plan of Newbury Borough circa 1840s *(NEBYM: 1961.21)*

a.   *Constable Beck (NEBYM:1979.72.374)*

b.   *Market Place Newbury (NEBYM: 1982.109.1)*

c.   *Canal Scene - West Mills (NEBYM: 1983.29.43)*

d.   *Early photograph of the Borough Fire Brigade (NEBYMI984.28.20)*

e.   *Newbury Theatre, Pelican Lane (NEBYM:T.164.2)*

f .   *Early drawing of London Road at its junction with The Broadway*
        (NEBYM: 1988.85.1)

g.   *Early photograph of Northbrook Street (NEBYM: 1985.9.1)*

h.   *1865 Board of Health notice (NEBYM: 1996.1 11.56)*

z.   *The Market Place - demonstration of a new fire escape ladder circa 1871*
        (NEBYM: 1979.72.318)

j.   *Button from early Police tunic (NEBYM:X. I14)*

k.   *Early truncheons and tipstaff (NEBYM: 1950.15) (NEBYM1938.280)*
        (NEBYM: 1964.29.1)

l.   *Photograph of Mansion House as it looked in the latter days of the*
    Borough Force (NEBYM2004.50.133)

m.   *Tipstaff thought to have been issued to Alfred Mils om, the first*
    Chief Constable (NEBYM: 1922.13)

n.   *The Town stocks (NEBYM:T.219)*

o.   *Cell door from the original Jail (NEBYM: 1924.33)*

p.   *Handcuffs (NEBYM:I 943.49)*

All photographs, drawings and sketches published in this book are reproduced by kind permission of The Heritage Service, West Berkshire Museum, The Wharf, Newbury.

INTRODUCTION

My aim in writing this book has been to place on record the details of a long-forgotten, small, local police force which was in existence for 39 years from 1836 until 1875.

In the course of undertaking this task much additional information has come to light, filling in a number of gaps in the 19th century history of the Borough of Newbury. For example, a number of past written histories of the borough have, in my view at least, not really taken full account of the existence of this Force and the overall impression is often given that Newbury did not have an organised police force until the formation of the Berkshire County Constabulary in 1856 which, of course, is incorrect.

It is hoped that this work will add a little to the overall municipal history of the Borough of Newbury and acknowledges the existence of its past, hard-working servants, the Borough Police Officers.

CHAPTER ONE
HISTORICAL AND LEGAL BACKGROUND

In today's society we accept the Police as the primary element in respect of law enforcement issues, but historically it is a little surprising to think that truly professional policing has only been in existence in this country for about the past 200 years. In the capital the Bow Street Runners had been in existence for some time before this, but they only covered certain areas of London and the major approach roads to the capital. Prior to this time Law enforcement was basically parish based. In the rural areas order was maintained by unpaid Parish Constables who worked, as and when required, under the direct control of Justices of the Peace. These constables carried out their official duties in conjunction with their every day activities acting as law enforcement officers only when a specific situation arose. In larger towns and boroughs, the parish normally employed Watchmen. The whole system varied enormously from area to area, not only as to how it was financed, but also in terms of organisation and general efficiency.

As a result of these limited and somewhat haphazard resources it became a fairly common practice in the late 18th and early 19th centuries for a number of ' self-help' societies to be formed throughout the country for the purpose of arresting and prosecuting thieves and felons. Newbury had such a society which had been formed as early as 1819 and was called 'The Newbury Association for the Apprehension of Thieves and Felons' . Although membership was open to any person living in Newbury or the immediate area, in practice, membership was limited to the more wealthy and property-owning members of the local community. In its early years the society's annual subscription fee was one guinea. In practice these societies did not provide an investigating service but, when the offender was both known and traceable, they did provide a prosecution service through the local society's solicitor. They would also pay the expenses of a parish constable required to act on their behalf. These societies, though strictly private organizations acting on behalf of their members, would have been able to offer monetary rewards for

1

information.

In the early years of the 19th century numerous changes were taking place throughout the country. many as a direct result of the Industrial Revolution, which brought about a general movement in the population and resulted in a more urban-based society, especially in the north due to the growth of the large industrial centres, which overall made for a more fluid and mobile society. In addition to these changes, in the early part of the century thousands of ex-soldiers were discharged from the army following the end of the Napoleonic Wars. The employment market could not absorb such large numbers and high unemployment caused many veterans to take to the road and often to a life of crime.

As a result of the Industrial Revolution many changes were taking place in working practices, both in the main manufacturing industries and within the agriculture industry. The country suffered a number of serious disturbances during the latter part of the 18th century and the early years of the 19th century. The serious 'Gordon Riots' which had taken place in 1780 and 1831 , saw a number of overtly political urban riots in such widely spaced places as Bristol, Derby and Nottingham. In the south, covering most of the southern counties roughly on a line from The Wash to the Bristol Channel, there occurred what have since become known as the 'Swing Riots', in which arson and machine breaking were the most public expressions of deep rooted anger amongst the farm labourers and the rural poor. It is generally accepted that the 'Swing Riots ' resulted from the development of various items of farm machinery and the consequent loss of traditional farming jobs. The new type of threshing machine was the main target of the rioters, as up until this time all threshing had been done by hand, with a flail , and this was the main source of winter employment for the average farm worker, but the advent of a new mechanised threshing machine put many out of work and became the rioters' main target. When it is considered that many of these labourers were practically on the bread-line to start with, being without work meant going on ' Parish Relief and in many cases, going to the dreaded 'workhouse' was the only alternative.

All these disturbances had been dealt with by the government in the traditional way by a show of force, mainly by using the army or hastily sworn in Special Constables. The army, either in the form of regulars or the militia, was the only disciplined force available to control serious civil disorder. Experience had shown however, that the means employed by the army could be very heavy-handed and overall this system had failed to contain the problems encountered.

In one form or other these methods had been adopted to deal with the 'Swing Riots'. In addition Special Assizes had been specifically set up to deal with the rioters, resulting in fairly severe sentences being handed out and this showed a clear indication of the government's determination to stamp out the insurrection. On the other hand the speed with which the 'Swing Riots' spread and the difficulties encountered by local magistrates in containing the disturbances, raised very real doubts in the minds of the government of the day as to whether or not the old traditional methods of controlling disorder were sufficient to contain the current problems. The county of Berkshire was one of the worst affected by the ' Swing' disturbances and the town of Newbury was very much the centre of such activity in West Berkshire. The local magistrates were obliged to swear in numerous men to act as Special Constables and they even had to call for military assistance in order to contain the outbreaks in the surrounding areas.

Throughout this period the country's national and local leaders grew increasingly concerned about crime and public order problems and the urgent need to do something positive about them. There had also been revolution, or the threat of it amongst our continental neighbours and our national leaders feared that these revolutionary ideas might spread across the channel. (This was certainly one of the fears during the 'Swing Riots '). There were also very active movements within this country demanding parliamentary reform. All these factors caused much debate in parliamentary circles about the possible introduction of a fully paid, professional, national police force.

Between 1829 and 1856 Parliament passed a series of Acts which effectively brought into being the 'New Police '. The process was a complex one surrounded by controversy at the time and subject to much debate later. The first of these acts was the Metropolitan Police Act, 1829, which, as the name suggests, created the Metropolitan Police and in fact the first Metropolitan Officers were patrolling the streets of London by September, 1829. Although it was considered that London was a special case, it was generally accepted that the crime and public order problems were nationwide and required urgent attention and, for the next few years, much discussion took place in parliament regarding the formation of properly organised Police Forces.

The main acts of parliament dealing with these issues after the 1829 Act, which just covered the metropolis, were 'The Lighting and Watching Act, 1833 ', which enabled Vestries to appoint an Inspector, who could in turn employ paid Watchmen. (Vestries were groups who acted as representatives of the local rate payers: a forerunner to Parish Councils, these groups invariably met in the vestry at the church, hence their name.) It is not possible to say how extensively this Act was used. It is clear, however, that in some areas it provided a useful way forward towards the concept of a paid Police Force. Newbury Borough, for example, employed Watchmen prior to the formation of its own Force.

The next major Act of Parliament dealing with the creation of Police Forces was the Municipal Corporations Act, 1835, which required all chartered Boroughs to form their own Police Forces funded from the rates. It was under this Act that the Borough Council of Newbury formed its own force, as did many other boroughs within Berkshire County. (It should be remembered that the Berkshire County Police Force did not come into existence until 1856, some twenty years later.) The Boroughs within Berkshire who formed their own forces at this time; were Abingdon (1836 - 1889), Maidenhead (1836 - 1889), Newbury (1836- 1875), New Windsor (1836- 1947), Wallingford (1836- 1856), Wantage (1828- 1856, prior to the formation of the Metropolitan Force) and Reading (1836- 1968). The second date in brackets shown against each force is the date when the force concerned was amalgamated with the Berkshire County Force, or in the case of Reading, the Thames Valley Police. It will be noted that two of the Boroughs, Wantage and Wallingford, joined the county force as soon as it was formed in 1856. New Windsor retained its own force until just after the Second World War and was amalgamated with the County Force when there were large scale Force amalgamations country wide in 1947. Reading, being the largest of the Borough Forces within Berkshire, retained its independence until the large scale amalgamations in 1968, when it was one of the five forces joined together to create the Thames Valley Police (Buckinghamshire, Berkshire, Oxfordshire, Oxford City and Reading Borough).

As previously mentioned, the majority of the rural areas outside the boroughs in 1836 were still being policed by the unreformed parochial system with the use of unpaid parish constables. This situation did not change in Berkshire until parliament introduced the compulsory County and Borough Police Act, 1856, requiring all county areas to provide full professional Police Forces. It was under this Act that the Berkshire County Constabulary was created, and it remained in existence until 1968 when it joined the other forces previously mentioned to form the Thames Valley Police.

However, we are now getting a little in advance of ourselves concerning dates. Although the County and Borough Police Act of 1856 is the major piece of legislation regarding the compulsory formation of county police forces, it is the Municipal Corporations Act of 1835 which allowed the creation of numerous Borough Police Forces throughout the country including the Borough of Newbury. This was a very far-sighted and far-reaching piece of legislation and its purpose was to modernise and standardise municipal corporations in England and Wales. The Act repealed all previous Acts, Charters and Customs which were found to be inconsistent with it and covered various issues on voting, both in parliamentary and local elections. It allowed for the employment of paid officials within the council, such as the Clerk, Treasurer, etc. and even allowed for full-time paid stipendiary Magistrates if the town was large enough to employ such an official. Under this Act Boroughs considered large enough could have their own court of Quarter Sessions and employ their own Recorder to adjudicate at the court. (Newbury had its own court of Quarter Sessions prior to this time). The Act also allowed for Boroughs to have their own jails, houses of correction, etc. (Here again Newbury had its own jail for a time). The Act also authorised the Borough to appoint its own Justices of the Peace. (An interesting point in respect of JPs is that, if they were appointed within a borough, they need not be qualified by reason of estate, as was the case in the county areas at that time.) The new councils were also allowed to make local bylaws, but from a law and order point of view, the most interesting part of the Act dealt with 'Watching' and allowed the borough councils to appoint Watch Committees, consisting of the Mayor and Councillors and this committee was able to appoint constables thus forming their own local force. It was also decreed that all such constables should also be sworn in as County Constables, enabling them to exercise their duties inside the county area within seven miles of any part of the borough, this radius also included any adjoining counties.

The Watch Committee was also obliged to make orders and regulations for the management of the force and was required to act as the disciplinary authority for the force. The Act itself also authorised the constables' powers, both in respect of arrests and taking bail recognizance and prescribed the penalty for assaulting a constable. All in all it was a far-sighted and far-reaching piece of legislation especially as far as policing was concerned.

The schedule to the actual Act lists all the various boroughs within England and Wales and the intentions of the Act in respect of each borough; for Newbury it is described as being *'an Act for lighting, watching, paving, cleansing and improving the streets, highways and places within the Borough, Town and Parish of Newbury and the Tithing or Hamlet of Speenhamland in the Parish of Speen in the County of Berkshire'.*

Having established the general background to the formation of police forces by the various municipal boroughs, the following account is a history of the Newbury Borough Police Force, which remained in existence for 39 years until its amalgamation with the Berkshire County Force in 1875 .

However, before embarking on a general account of the formation of the Newbury Borough Police, it would be as well to reflect on the state of the Borough of Newbury in the 1830's and 1840's in order to appreciate the sort of problems which might have faced the newly formed borough police. Comparative to today's figures the population was small, but Newbury was nevertheless a bustling, busy and vibrant little town, boasting the largest corn market in the whole of the country.

The 1831 census showed a population of just 5,967. In addition, the surrounding parishes of Speen (pop. 3,044), Shaw (pop. 620), and Greenham (pop. 1061) would surely have increased the town's daytime population as the chances are that a significant number of men residing in these immediate adjoining parishes were likely to have been employed within the actual borough.

It would be reasonable to assume that the coaching and canal trades accounted for a large number of itinerant workers who would not have been included in the census. The large volume of coach and long distance wagon traffic to and from all points east and west - London to Bath and Bristol - and north and south - Winchester, Oxford, Andover, Salisbury and the Midlands - must have made the Speenhamland area in particular an extremely vibrant place.

The whole area must have been seething with horse-drawn traffic and the fact that it was the midway and overnight transit point between London and Bath gave the town an extra special flavour. Bearing in mind that, in the main, coach travellers were likely to come from the more affluent sections of society, one can well imagine that this area of the town had a great attraction for the more criminally minded members of the community such as conmen, pickpockets, fraudsters and thieves in general, to say nothing of the ranks of the oldest female profession, who, without doubt, would have found the pickings very good amongst large numbers of the travelling public, who were in most cases obliged to stay overnight.

The large coaching inns in Speenhamland were very prosperous establishments and it is recorded that the largest of them all, the 'Pelican', had stabling facilities for up to 300 horses. When one takes into account the number of grooms, ostlers, stable lads and general workers required to look after these numbers, one can form an idea of the scale of traffic involved in the coaching industry. These facilities related to just one establishment, albeit the largest, but there were numerous others involved in the coaching trade in this part of the town.

The theatre in Speenhamland, appears to have been very popular with the travelling public and with the more affluent sections of the local population. In addition to the large coaching inns in and around Speenhamland, there were numerous other taverns and public houses within the borough. The records for 1844 show a total of 52 taverns and public houses within the actual borough limits, plus 27 beer houses. In addition to the continuous daily coach traffic passing through the Borough the canal brought much barge traffic. At this time the canal company itself was operating a daily service (except Sundays) of goods barges from the town wharf to both London and Bristol. ADEY's barges were operating on a weekly basis from the West Mills Wharf to Bath, Bristol, Bradford, Devizes, Swindon and Trowbridge. FLINT's boats were doing likewise on a weekly basis, operating from the main town wharf. Apart from these locally based companies there were numerous other 'through ' boats using the canal, including a number of daily 'Fly Boats' which carried passengers as well as freight.

In the early 1840's a new system of public transport appeared on the scene in Newbury with the coming of the railways, and although the railway itself would not present a problem for law and order, the actual construction of it must have created a lot of problems for the local police force in coping with-the vast army of navvies who must have descended on the area to build the railways. One can begin to assess the possible effects on a small town of the arrival of these hard-working, hard-drinking and hard-living men. Their only outlet for any sort of pleasure would have been the local taverns and beer houses, with any ancillary entertainment in the form of female company which could be provided.

Taking all these factors into consideration one soon begins to realise that to be employed as a Police Officer at this time was certainly no sinecure, the more so as he was expected to work seven days a week with no day off and the days were long. They obviously imposed their presence by force, and no doubt were obliged, at times, to meet violence with violence. There was no political correctness 'clap-trap' to bother with, and although at times the old watchmen in particular have been held up as persons of ridicule, they must have been men of above average ability when it came to enforcing the law as to do so at this time would have required a fair amount of bravery on their part, as they operated very much on their own, with no immediate ' back-up' with wireless communication, etc.

It was against this general background that the force was formed.

CHAPTER TWO
THE FORMATION OF THE FORCE ~
APPOINTMENT OF THE FIRST CHIEF CONSTABLE
AND OTHER OFFICERS

The transformation from the old night watch system in Newbury to the new Borough Police began on Friday, 22 January, 1836 at a full meeting of the Borough Council, which consisted of Aldermen Slocock and Satchell and Councillors Flint, Gray, Bunny, James, Payne, E. W. Gray, Kimber, Vincent, Trumplett, Dredge and Shaw. The Mayor, Mr. John Alexander, was in the chair. It was moved and seconded, and carried unanimously that, at the next meeting of the Council, the whole Council would form itself into a Watch Committee, in accordance with Section 76 of the Municipal Corporations Act, 1835.

At a subsequent meeting on 5 February 1836 it was agreed that a sub-committee be formed for the purpose of carrying out the provisions of Section 76 into execution and the following gentlemen of the council be formed into that sub-committee:- Messrs. Flint, Satchel!, Slocock, Trumplett and E. W. Gray. At a further meeting on 12 February, two additional members, Messrs. James and Kimber, were elected to this working party committee.

This sub-committee appears to have been a hard working group of men, as they subsequently presented their report to the Watch Committee (The full Borough Council) at a meeting on Wednesday, 17 February, 1836. (The full text of this report is shown at Appendix 1.) The report was concise, but it covered all aspects for the basic foundation of the new force and also gives an insight into the old 'Night Watch' system. (It appears that prior to 1836 Newbury had a regular 'Night Watch' system, which had for many years been operated by Commissioners under a local Act for the improvement of the Borough). The old 'Night Watch' consisted of one night constable and four watchmen. There was no day-time Police establishment at all, and the sub-committee drew the Council's attention to this fact. The report refers to shoals of beggars, itinerant tradesmen, Match women and boys infesting the Borough daily, and there being no regular daytime Police to regulate them and control them.

The sub-committee gave a breakdown of the wages and general running expenses of the old system and their recommendations for the new establishment. They also recommended various persons for the posts of Chief Constable, Beadle, Assistant Beadle and Night Constable, and these recommendations were subsequently adopted by the Watch Committee, at a meeting on 29 February, 1836. However, at the meeting of the full council it was agreed to increase the wages of Alfred Milsom, the Chief Constable elect to £1 per week, and that his pay should commence on 1.3.36. It was also decided that the Beadle, John Wallen and the Assistant Beadle, Henry Beck should also commence their duties on the same date, receiving a weekly wage of 4/- and 8/6d per week respectively. (It appears that the council minutes may have transposed these two amounts as it would seem unlikely that the Beadle's wage would have been lower than that of his assistant.) At this meeting the council also arranged for another sub-committee to be appointed for the purposes of framing rules and regulations for the guidance and direction of the Chief Constable and Beadles, and for carrying into execution the full provisions of Section 76 of the Municipal Corporations Act, 1835. This second sub-committee consisted of Messrs. Payne, Shaw, Trumplett, Kimber and E. W. Gray. Also at this full council meeting it was decided to appoint William Langton as Night Constable and Joseph Allen, Isaac Weston, David King and Edward Wilder as Watchmen. All these men had in fact been employed on the Town Night Watch prior to this time.

Here again the appointed sub-committee did not waste much time, as within two weeks they had reported back to the council on their findings, producing a report and a manuscript handbill for display and publication for the information of the ratepayers and general inhabitants of Newbury, on the formation and general role of the new Police Force. With the exception of a few minor amendments the manuscript handbill is identical to the full notice which was subsequently published and is shown in full at Appendix 2. Newbury in common with the times appears to have had its share of disorderly persons, beggars, drunks and lewd and common women. The notice also informed the public of the basic rules and regulations governing the new force and the manner in which the complaints against the force could be made. Here again it was a very professional and workmanlike document.

The sub-committee also reported to the council that in accordance with directives previously given they had ordered the necessary clothing for the day police. There appears to have been a slight problem in the changeover period from the old Night Watch as no wages had been paid to the Night Constable and the four Watchmen for a week and neither had the Night Constable been paid for the oil and coal used during this period in the Watch House. These matters were eventually resolved amicably. (One gets the impression that the commissioners under the old system were also councillors within the new town council) and not withstanding this, these kinds of problems could easily arise today when whole systems are changed over. In addition to the draft notice, the sub-committee also prepared a most detailed report on the future duties of the Police (see Appendix 3 for the full report) and one of the most far-reaching recommendations in this report was a suggestion that a committee of managers be set up within the Watch Committee and that each manager would be in charge of the day-to-day running of the force on a weekly basis. This recommendation was subsequently adopted in 1837 and operated for a number of years and it can be seen that the force was very much a local affair and well and truly under the direct control of the locally elected councillors. *(See page 18 for further details.)*

Little is known of the background of the newly appointed officers but there is a mention in the records of the Newbury Borough Quarter Sessions on 13 January 1826, some ten years prior to the formation of the force, of Alfred Milsom, who is described as being a Patrolman, and during the execution of his duties as such, being assaulted by one George Lloyd. There is another mention of him being assaulted whilst in the execution of his duty by a 'Bargeman' in 1827.

The word 'Patrolman ' appears to indicate that he was in charge of the Night Watch at the time of these incidents and, as he was selected as the new Chief Constable of the Borough, one assumes that he had some background in law enforcement. He was also the duly appointed Beadle and Bellman for the Borough from at least 1829 to 1831 and this position in itself carried a semi-quasi law enforcement role. Recently acquired information suggests that Mr.

Milsom was involved as a 'Law Enforcement Officer' during the mass arrests that took place in the Newbury area following the 'Swing Riots ' of 1830.

John Wallen, the Beadle and Bellman, was nick-named the 'DogRapper' and he had previously combined the duties of Parish Beadle and Town Crier. He is described as wearing a cocked hat and a coat with voluminous capes, carrying a formidable staff with a brass knob at the end. One also assumes that Henry Beck, a native of Reading, was previously employed in very much the same capacity as Beadle and Bill Sticker, prior to the formation of the new force. After the changeover both the Beadles were involved in more law-enforcement issues, although Beck appears to have retained many of his old duties, and one gets the impression that he was also used as a general factotum for the council, over and above his Police duties.

The Night Constable, William Langton, had been in charge of the old 'Night Watch ' immediately prior to the formation of the new force. The four Watchmen, Messrs. Allen, Weston, King and Wilder, had all been employed as Night Watchmen under the old system. It is also interesting to note that at least two of these men, Messsrs. Allen and King, were unable to write their names, as on a subsequent petition which the Night Officers submitted to the Watch Committee requesting an increase in wages, they could only make a mark 'X' instead of a signature.

In practice the only two persons who could really be classified as police officers, as we know them today, would be the Chief Constable, Alfred Milsom and the Night Constable, William Langton.

It is doubtful if the actual transition from the old watch system to the 'New Police' was particularly noticeable to the average inhabitant of the Borough, as the same men were more or less employed in carrying out the same duties as previously, except more emphasis was placed on patrolling the beats and there was now a day time police. The major change of course, was in respect of control and accountability, which was now completely in the hands of the local Borough Council.

The birth of the modem Police Force had taken place within the Borough of Newbury.

It is of interest to note that most of the Borough authorities within the county of Berkshire took the opportunity at this time to form their own Forces under the authority of the Municipal Corporations Act of 1835. The Act itself can be viewed as one of the first major pieces of legislation to cover law enforcement issues, thereby laying the basic foundation stones of the modem concept of policing.

This was the general background to the formation of the Newbury Borough Police Force.

CHAPTER THREE
THE FIRST FIVE YEARS ~ 1836 - 1840
JAIL BREAKS ~ DISMISSAL OF NIGHT CONSTABLE
BABY'S BODY IN BASKET
WATCH COMMITTEE ~ MANAGERS

The Force made its first real appearance on 26 March, 1836. As stated earlier, there was a slight problem regarding the payment of the officers as the Commissioners, under the old night watch scheme, ceased paying for the town watch a week before the new Force came into existence causing serious concern to the officers involved. The new Borough Council, to its credit, decided to backdate the wages by a week so that the men would not be out of pocket, although strictly speaking it was not their problem, as the night watch was still employed by the old Borough Commissioners.

The ' Day police' were issued with 'stove pipe' type hats, a plain blue frock coat, dark blue trousers and a black stock. The stock was usually made of leather, about 4 inches in depth, often fastened with a buckle and protected the wearer from being garrotted or strangled from behind. (From about 1875 the stock became an integral part of the tunic, with a small tab of patent leather sewn inside the collar.) The Nightwatchmen were issued with broad brimmed hats, stocks, watch coats, trousers and capes. The drawing on the front cover of this book is a copy of an original held in the town museum, showing Henry Beck in his full uniform bearing some sort of insignia on the collar. The tall stove pipe hat is in keeping with the general headgear adopted in most early police forces and was generally reinforced with stiff leather to give some protection to the wearer. The Chief Constable's badge of office was a small baton or tipstaff, which is on display in the town museum. All other officers were issued with staves, rattles, lamps and lanthornes.

Once the new force was up and running, the Watch Committee submitted a detailed report to the Home Secretary of the day, Lord Russell, informing him of the exact details of the force, strength, pay, duties and responsibilities, etc. (see appendix 4) It is of interest to note that the unpaid parish constables and the tythingmen were still in existence at this time, and they actually get a special mention in the last paragraph of this report.

The Borough Police Station together with limited cell accommodation was situated in the Town Hall in Mansion House Street. At this time the Borough also had its own jail in Cheap Street, which was almost on the spot and, until recently, had been occupied by the library, but prisoners would have been admitted to this establishment only after being convicted or remanded in custody prior to a full court hearing. (The jail is thought to have been large enough to accommodate between 30-40 prisoners). It will be seen from the suggested duties shown in the Sub Committee's report (Appendix 3) that, in common with the times the new Police were expected to carry a fairly heavy workload and be available at all times- no days off are mentioned. This was the normal practice throughout the country in the early days of the 'New' Police.

A request in the form of a petition was received by the Watch Committee from the Night Constables in May, 1836, requesting additional wages: -

'To the Worshipful Mayor and Watch Committee of the Borough of Newbury, assembled. We the undersigned, constituting the Night Watch of the said Borough, assembled herewith. That they wish to state for the consideration of your honourable committee, that they all have large families entirely dependant on them and that in the summer months there is 5/- taken off their weekly stipend, leaving but barely sufficient for the support of our humble petitioners alone, and not having any other employment during the day whereby they may add to the support of their families, being considered in your employ entirely. Most humbly beggeth that your honourable committee will take it into your consideration and enhance their summer stipend and should it please your honourable committee that our duty should commence at an earlier hour, your petitioners will cheerfully and strictly comply with every order that your honourable committee may deem necessary to issue for the guidance and government of the night Police establishment. Hoping that our humble petition may meet with your approbation, your petitioners in duty bound will ever pray.

Signed: W. Langton - Night Constable.
Josh Alien 'X' His Mark. David King 'X' His Mark. Edward
Wilder and Isaac Weston. (Watchmen)'
(Reproduced by kind permission of the Berkshire Record Office -
N/Ac2/1/1)

The records show that this petition was received, taken into due consideration and, to the Committee's credit, it was agreed that the additional payment of 2/6d per week should be made to each of the Watchmen and to the Night Constable during the summer season, and that they be required to be on duty from 10 o'clock at night to 4am. It was also agreed at this meeting that a rate should be declared for the Borough so as to incorporate the expenses of the new Borough Police Force in the form of a ' Watch Rate' of 9d. in the pound.

Poor David King, one of the Night Watchmen, did not enjoy his additional pay for long as he died on 12 August, 1836 and one John Tomkins was appointed in his place. During this period the Watch Committee issued new foul weather capes to the members of the 'Night Patrol ' . In general the equipment issued by the Watch Committee / Borough Council appears to have been of a good quality, and the Council undertook the cleaning and repair of the garments at regular intervals, which suggests that the authorities tried to run the Force from the outset in an efficient and businesslike manner.

The Force as a whole appears to have progressed well without undue problems for the next few months, but in November, 1836 the Watch Committee was faced with a law and order issue, but not one that directly involved the new force,. The incident itself involved an escape from the town jail of a prisoner who, in the process of making his escape, also stole all the jail keys. During this period, in addition to having its own police force, the Borough ran its own jail facility which was situated next to the workhouse in Cheap Street, more or less on the site occupied by the library until 2000. The jail was used to house convicted offenders and persons on remand. The overnight Police Cells were in the Police Station, within the Town Hall in Mansion House Street. (For a plan of the Borough Jail, see Appendix 5).

The escapee was one Jonathan Perry, who made good his escape by knocking down the gaoler, a man called Samuels. The incident appears to have occurred when his cell was opened up to give him a meal and there is no record of Perry ever being recaptured. This incident obviously caused much interest in the Borough and resulted in the submission of numerous reports by the Chief Constable and alterations and changes of locks to all the cell doors. It was also decided by the Watch Committee that William Langton, the Night Constable, should move his abode and take up temporary residence with his family in the workhouse so that in future he could be on hand to assist with additional security, should it be required, during the daytime. It also appears that Langton had been of some assistance in frustrating a previous attack on the Jail Keeper. The other recommendations made as a result of this escape were that the Jailer, Samuels, should sleep at the workhouse near the jail, or that he should find a person to do so on his behalf. (One assumes that, prior to this time, the prisoners were just locked in their cells overnight with no-one in authority remaining on the premises.) Alterations to cell doors, providing flaps for the passage of food and drinks without having to open the doors, were made. It is of interest to note that the Watch Committee stipulated that the hatches had to be large enough to take a quart cup and a plate with eatables upon it. Another suggestion was that all convicted prisoners should be issued with suits of partly coloured clothing.

The instructions issued regarding William Langton 's place of residence imply that the Watch Committee wielded a fair amount of authority over its Force members.

The subject of jail security arose again a few weeks later with a further escape of two inmates. The records do not show exactly how they got out, but the subsequent report and recommendations make for interesting reading:

'In consequence of notice received from the Mayor on 16 March, 1837, a survey and inspection was made of the prison and the following recommendations made so as the prison can be made secure, before the Quarter Sessions are held on Tuesday, 4 April, 1837.

1. *It was proposed that two strong iron bars be affixed to the planks fastened against the North walls of the cells 2, 3 & 4 that such bars run the whole length of the cells and that iron bolts be introduced, to be*

carried entirely through the wall and made secure on
the outside by a nut screwed on a piece of iron of
about a foot in length.

2. We suggest that straps of iron hoop be nailed or
screwed on the ceilings over all the privys, such straps
being about a yard or four feet long.

3. We recommend that in cell number 7 (being the cell
from whence the prisoners attended to in Mayor's
notice escaped, the plank by which the ceiling is
secured be removed for the purposes of introducing a
new plank to run the entire length of the cell, or to
replace the plank removed by the prisoners on their
escape, and to secure same by strong iron straps.

4. We recommend that shutters be placed over the
boards before the windows in cells 1, 7 & 9 and that
the same be secured on the outside by lock or bolt, or
that the shutters at present within the cells be repaired
and put into a state of security, in order to prevent
prisoners making the hinges attached to same into
instruments by which they may find the means (as in
the recent instance) of effecting their escape.

*Having recommended in our first report of 14 February last that Langton, the
Night Constable, should stay over one or other of the cells, we were not aware that he
or someone of his family did so, until we found that the contrary was the fact, after
the escape of the two prisoners, who gained their liberty since the date of the original
report.

(Reproduced by kind permission of the Berkshire Record OfficeN/
Ac.2/1/l)*

It appears that the prisoners made good their escape by removing part of the
building fabric and the subsequent recommendations give a clear impression
that the actual structure of the building from a security viewpoint left a lot to
be desired.

Presumably as a direct result of the recent escapes, the Watch Committee obviously thought that their control over the new Police and the Borough Jail needed to be tightened up, and at a meeting of the full Watch committee on 20 February 1837 the following motion was agreed upon:

'That a sub committee of four or five members of the watch committee be appointed and to be called, 'The Managers of the Police' each of whom shall in weekly terms take the control and the superintendency of the day and night police and that the said managers in conjunction with the mayor do prepare a set of rules for the management of the said police, and report the same to the watch committee for their approval in time to be transmitted to the Secretary of State, previous to the 1st April, and that the nomination of the sub committee be postponed to the next meeting of the Watch Committee.'

(Reproduced by kind pennission of the Berkshire Record Office- N/Ac.2/1/ I)

This recommendation was subsequently agreed and taken into use. The first sub committee of managers consisted of Messrs. Shaw, Payne, Kimber and Gray, and it was agreed that they should remain in office acting as managers and rotating on a weekly basis to 12 May, 1837, when a further four members of the Watch Committee, would serve as managers in their place for the following quarter. This particular arrangement went on for a number of years whilst the new force was in its infancy, and one can well imagine that the 'Weekly Managers' wielded considerable power and were in effect more in charge of the force than the Chief Constable. (See Appendix 6 for full details of the report and duties of the 'Managers').

At a meeting of the Watch Committee on 18 March, 1837 the question arose as to whether or not the Night Constable Langton was actually sleeping in the workhouse above the cells as designated, so they directed that Henry Cook do so in future in order to give more security to the town jail. (It is not certain who Cook was as there is no mention of him holding a position in the Police).

The new Night Watchman, John Tompkins, managed to 'blot his copybook' soon after joining the force: at a meeting of the Watch Committee on 1 April 1837 it was ordered that he should be seen by the Mayor in order to be admonished and warned to be more circumspect in the future following a complaint made against him for using some ' unguarded expressions ' whilst drinking in the Pigeons Beer House.

In April the Council sent a full report to the Home Secretary of the day, Lord John Russell, outlining the Force's progress since its formation twelve months previously. It was stated that the Force had given general satisfaction and that there had been a general decrease in felonies since its inception. John Wallen retired from the Force In July, 1837 on age grounds having been given the promise of an almshouse. (No question of early retirement in those days.) One William Stroud was appointed in his place as Bellman and Policeman, his salary being 8/- per week and any additional fees which he might receive attached to the use of the bell. Unfortunately this gentleman did not serve long in this office as, on 21 March 1838, the Watch Committee received his letter of resignation, his reason being that he considered the pay to be inadequate. As there was no candidate awaiting consideration for the appointment, the Watch Committee agreed to advertise the position and had a notice as shown below posted in the Mansion House.

BOROUGH OF NEWBURY

Notice is hereby given that the Watch committee of the borough, being the council thereof, will meet on Tuesday evening the 3rdApril next for the purpose of electing a Bel/man and Policeman in the room of William Stroud, resigned. Candidates for the office may ascertain the terms and the particulars of the duties required to be performed by application to Alfred Milsom, Chief Constable.

(Signed) E. W. Gray
Secretary of the Watch Committee
Newbury, 22 March, 1838.
(Reproduced by kind permission of the Berkshire Record Office- N/Ac.2/1/1)

On 3 April, 1838 the Committee appointed one William Gatehouse as Bell man and Police Officer in place of the departed Stroud and, *once again,* this appointment was short-lived as it was subsequently reported by the Watch Committee that Gatehouse had been neglectful in his duties. He was admonished by the Mayor, told to be more circumspect in his conduct and was warned that any repetition could lead to his dismissal. On this understanding he was allowed to continue in office, but the records show that, within a day or so, he had submitted his resignation. His term in office had lasted only a few weeks and there is no record of the nature of his neglect.

At the same meeting the Watch Committee decided to stop the practice of giving Constables and Jurymen a one shilling fee for their duties at Coroners' Inquests, as it was generally spent on the premises, resulting in what is, delicately described as 'consequence unbecoming'. It was customary to conduct inquests on licensed premises and the Watch Committee hoped that the money saved by withholding the shilling fee would not only cover the cost of hiring a larger, more suitable room for the purpose, but would also prevent the sometimes boisterous behaviour of those who spent their shillings' in the bar immediately the proceedings were over.

In accordance with the normal practice quarterly reports were submitted to the Home Secretary giving an up-date on the general progress of the newly created Force. Around this time a report was submitted pointing out that there were only two prisoners for trial at the next borough Quarter Sessions, both on trivial charges, one for stealing a piece of calico and the other for stealing a pair of shoes. In both cases the aggrieved was the union workhouse. These two were the only prisoners committed on charges of felony within the borough during the previous half year. It was then stated that, prior to the establishment of the new Force, the average number of prisoners sent for trial at the County Sessions had always been between four and six. The drop in prisoner numbers was put down to the presence of the new Force bringing a visible presence of law and order to the streets of the Borough. In view of the settled state of the Borough, the Watch Committee decided that it was not necessary to replace Officer Stroud. The official explanation for the reduction of authorised strength was that 'The Borough had settled into a quiet and peaceful state since the introduction of the new system of Policing '. (One wonders how many present day Police Committees could make such a claim.)

Throughout the remainder of 1838 nothing of any great importance involving the force appears to have taken place. However, the Chief Constable, Alfred Milsom, did not share the Watch Committee's enthusiasm at losing one of his officers and made a couple of requests, to no avail, to have this decision reversed.

The only other item of interest recorded during the latter part of the year was that the Watchmen's coats were in a pitiable state, resulting in the Watch Committee ordering four new coats.

At a meeting of the Watch Committee on 2 April, 1839 it is of interest to note that they discussed a petition which appears to have been circulated to Borough Forces nationwide regarding a possible amalgamation of the City of London Police with the Metropolitan Force. This suggestion has been raised by central government many times over the intervening years. The Newbury Watch Committee was concerned that this line could also be applied to other local forces throughout the country, thus placing too much power into the hands of the executive, in this case, the central government. As a result they voted against such a merger, and the mayor affixed the Borough Seal to the official reply to this effect.

On 18 June, 1839 the Watch Committee received a further request from the night officers requesting an increase in wages during the summer months and the records show that the night constables had gathered together numerous signatures from what is recorded as 'Respectable inhabitants of the town ' in support of their claim. It was subsequently decided to refer the whole question of pay, for both the day and night establishment, to a sub-committee to investigate and report accordingly. They must have reported favourably as the pay of the night police was increased from 30 June 1839 and their hours of duty were also amended from 9pm until 6am during the remaining months of the year. There appears to have been a change of heart by the committee over the question of William Langton (the Night Constable) and the requirement that he should live at the workhouse in order to be in a position to assist with security during the day at the town jail, as now he was formally given seven days' notice to quit these premises. It is of interest to note that around this time, the council officially praised the Police on duty at one of the town fairs for keeping crime down. There is also mention in the records of a gang of mostly female shoplifters operating in the town, but there is no mention of whether or not they were apprehended.

The remainder of the year appears to have passed off without undue problems. However, at a meeting of the Watch Committee on 22nd May, 1840, the Mayor reported that William Langton had been charged with stealing straw from the cattle market and on being examined had admitted the charge. After making enquiries to establish the facts, the Watch Committee resolved that Langton be removed immediately from his situation and that his place be filled at some future date. It was subsequently agreed to place an advertisement in the Reading newspapers for a Superintendent of the Night Police at a salary of £52.0.0 per annum. There is no record of Langton appearing before a court so it is assumed that, other than losing his job, no further action was taken against him for this seemingly trivial affair.

In May, 1840 the Police were faced with a very strange case involving the body of a baby girl which had been sent in a basket on the Optimus Coach from London . An inquest was held at the Speenhamland Committee Room by the Coroner, J. Bunny Esquire. The Coachman, a Mr. Robert Neyler, gave evidence to the effect that the basket , having been pre-booked, was given into his charge at the start of his journey at The White Horse Cellar, Piccadilly .. When he was subsequently informed of the basket's contents he made enquiries of the Coach company's book-keeper in London, but it appears that the book-keeper could not remember who brought the basket into the office in the first place. The basket was addressed to a Mrs. Green at Speen Hill, but as no person of that name lived there, it was taken to Mr. Green, a shoemaker of Speenhamland, who, on opening the basket, discovered its gruesome contents. The body was reportedly dressed in a night gown and cap, the wrists and bosom of which were sewn up. Mr. Green immediately contacted the Police who took possession of the basket and contents. Mr. R. Robinson, a surgeon, gave evidence that he had carried out a post mortem examination of the body and had discovered no marks of violence thereon, except some discolouration around the lips which might have been caused by the finger nails. In his opinion, the child had been born alive but had not lived long. The jury returned a verdict of ' Wilful murder against some person or persons unknown' . No details are available as to whether or not any further successful action was taken regarding this very strange case.

Throughout this period the local borough Magistrates' Court appears to have been kept reasonably busy; charges such as 'assault on police' were fairly common, plus the usual run of minor disturbances, breach of the peace and minor larcenies. The records show a number of cases brought against 'Runaway Husbands' who had deserted their wives and families and left them to be kept on the ' rates '. The local Borough Council, through its police department, put in a considerable amount of work trying to chase up these wayward men so as to ease the burden on the ratepayers, something of which modern day administrators might take note.

Although the following item has nothing to do with the police or general law enforcement, it has been included to give some idea of the Borough Council 's forward and humane thinking as it was in 1840. The Council sent a petition to central government with a view to stopping the use of young boys to climb chimneys for sweeping purposes. This action appears to have been taken following a public meeting in the town. After the meeting an association was formed to try to stop this abusive practice.

On 12 June, 1840, one George Deane was appointed Superintendent of the Night Police (note the new title). It was also agreed at the same meeting that Isaac Weston, one of the night patrolmen who had been in temporary charge of the night police since Langton's dismissal, should be paid an additional sum for this extra duty, increasing his wage to 12 shillings per week for the period in question .

Mr. Deane appears to have had a fairly extensive background in law enforcement duties having originally been employed as a Constable at Shinfield, and later serving as a Sergeant in the newly formed Reading Borough Police since its inception in 1836. It is interesting to note that Mr. Deane is not described as being a Sergeant with Newbury, but as a Superintendent in charge of the Night Police, a somewhat grand title when one compares it to today's Police rank structure. In the National Police and Constabulary published lists of 1844 he is shown as being Inspector and Assistant to the Chief Constable. One assumes that the rank of Inspector would be more appropriate as he had previously been a Sergeant in the Reading Force, so becoming an Inspector at Newbury was a promotion.

During the autumn months of 1840 an enquiry was set up by the Home Secretary. This arose from a complaint by Doctor Hibbert Binny, the Rector of Newbury, against the Mayor and Justices of the Borough regarding an increase in the rates levied on his property. Doctor Binny claimed that the Council had failed to legislate properly and therefore challenged the validity of the rateable value of his property. The enquiry was conducted on behalf of the Home Secretary by the Recorder of the Borough, Mr. Whately. One gets a clear impression that there was very little love lost between the parties involved. Doctor Binny made a total of eight complaints, among them he claimed a lack of courtesy from officials including the Police, who had been obliged to serve various official documents upon him as the complainant.

The allegations against the Mayor and Justices were dismissed, but it was decided that there should be a reduction in Doctor Binny's rates. The whole issue made national headlines with a full page report of the proceedings published in *The Times* in early November. Subsequent correspondence appeared on the letter pages of *The Times* as late as 28th December, 1840.

It is of interest to note that Doctor Binny's opening address to the Enquiry is said to have lasted for nearly six hours.

CHAPTER FOUR
1841-1845 THE FORMATIVE YEARS
RIOTS OVER 'ENCLOSURES, ETC.

It is of interest to note that in October 1841 the Watch Committee appointed a Mrs. Esther Frewin to act as Matron at the Borough Jail to attend solely on the female prisoners at a salary of 1/6d. per week. During this period a report was received from a subcommittee regarding the condition of the jail, and as a result it was decided that the jailer must reside at all times at the jail; it was also agreed that the system used up to this time, regarding the manner in which the food was purchased, should be abolished and a proper dietary table adopted, which should be printed in notice form and posted in each of the cells. Another decision was made that, in future, prisoners must be placed in separate beds, be housed one to a cell if possible, and not more than three to a cell. (One wonders about the situation prior to this order.) It was also ordered that the walls of the jail be scraped and whitewashed annually.

1842 was to be a memorable year for the borough as far as general law and order was concerned. The new force had its first real taste of a public order situation in September of that year, when serious disturbances occurred following a decision to enclose the two open fields within the Borough known as Eastfields and Westfields. Until this time town inhabitants had enjoyed more or less free access to these fields and were allowed to graze their cattle there once the corn or other crops had been harvested by the owners. This custom of winter grazing appears to have been enjoyed by all the freeholders and inhabitant householders of the borough, one presumes since time immemorial. It is fair to say that the enclosure question was a very emotive issue amongst the general inhabitants, but in the preceding years the privilege of grazing cattle on the common fields had probably been abused, as one assumes that the average borough householder no longer kept his own individual cattle as had been the case in earlier years. The persons who appeared to take advantage of this free grazing seem for the most part to have been horse dealers and others who had become temporary inhabitants of the borough merely for the purpose of enjoying and monopolising the benefits of what was described as the 'turn out', the free grazing.

Notwithstanding this, the general situation over the proposed enclosures was very complicated and the whole issue became very emotive, resulting in public disturbances. The Borough police, with the help of special constables, were actively involved in trying to keep the peace and numerous arrests were made. The main land owner of the Westfields, a Mr. R. F. Graham, subsequently issued a very lengthy memorandum addressed to all the inhabitants of the Borough outlining his version of the problems which had been encountered; he also included in this document various copies of legal advice which had been received in respect of the whole enclosure issue. To give some idea of the problems encountered by the landowners and police, a part of Mr. Graham's report is reproduced and reads as follows:

'I now come to the proceedings of the past week. It was on Friday last, the 23rd instant, that the recent disturbance commenced; it was in the evening of that day that Robert Aldridge and his partisans rushed from the city to the rescue of two of Aldridge 's horses which had been impounded, and, amidst oaths and imprecations, too foul to be repeated, committed the most dastardly assaults upon those men, who, in the execution of their Master 's legal and rightful orders, were quietly conveying those horses into the pound. That Aldridge was no occupier of the land, was in fact well known: that he was put forward at the head of a reckless mob as the champion of the respectable inhabitant householders of New bury, to fight for their alleged rights, was a supposition which I could not for a moment, entertain; however, from whatever causes he became the leader of that mob, I deemed it my duty to put myself in immediate communication with him, I lost not a moment in assuring him and his party, that, if they were contending for what they considered their rights, there was a plain, simply, manly, and straightforward manner in which they should seek to establish them, and that if they would take the course which the law pointed out to them, and bring the question before a legal tribunal, I would pay the costs of all parties be the verdict what it might: insults of the grossest kind were the only reply to my proposal, and finding that no conciliatory observations would prevail anything with a mob, for the most part in the highest state of excitement and drunkenness.

I retired from the scene, leaving Milsom (Chief Constable) to preserve the peace of the district; the further events of that evening and of Saturday I will not trouble you with, as I was not an eye witness to them, but, on the Sunday morning, matters had arrived at that pitch, when a regularly organised mob of many hundreds of the most dissolute and abandoned characters, began their work of devastation shortly before nine o 'clock. Having heard their movements I immediately went out to them, wholly unprotected, and in that manner one would have thought to disarm all violence on their part, there were apparently, but few persons assembled in the field, and those few were standing at the West End by the school. I had no sooner made my appearance in the field than it became the signal for assembling their force: Aldridge, Aberdeen, Piercey, Beckett and Adler were foremost in their ranks, they bore down upon me in a mob of many hundreds, with most terrific hooting and abuse, apparently ripe for every devastation, and wholly reckless of all consequences; still I thought it a duty I owed to the public as well as myself to meet them in a conciliatory tone, and begged of them, at all events, to suspend their measures for the Sunday; I repeated to them the offer I had made on the Friday evening, by which the right they claimed, might be brought to an issue without expense to them; I was answered only with violence and abuse, cursing and swearing, exceeding everything it had ever been my lot to sustain or hear, bludgeons were raised in all directions, and hooting and threatenings were continued, until, finding the mob mad in their career, I left them with the assurance, that no act of provocation whatever should 'proceed from my party during that day!

(Reproduced by kind permission of the Berkshire Record office - N/AP.4/33)

The local police were obviously very involved in this ongoing public order situation, which appears to have lasted for a number of days, if not longer, and resulted in a number of arrests being made.

When the general situation regarding the enclosure issue quietened down, the Borough Council formed a special committee to look into 'all the aspects of the fields in question as to the custom, usage, rights, etc.' This committee was also charged with arranging meetings with the landowners and charity trustees who had a vested interest in the common fields. The sub-committee reported back to the main council at a meeting held on 9 November, 1842.

It was subsequently proposed by Doctor Binney that before the meeting considered what action to take in respect of the common fields, it be made a preliminary that all proceedings against persons who had been charged with riot, assault and rescue in respect of the recent disturbances, 'be withdrawn and forever put an end to'. This motion was carried and the meeting expressed its thanks to Doctor Binney for his impartial conduct in the chair. (Doctor Binney appears to have been something of an 'Honest Broker' in this dispute, which had caused a lot of ill feeling amongst the general population of the Borough, and the decision to drop all charges appears to have helped to heal the wounds). The enclosure question appears to have rumbled on in one form or another until 1846, when approval was finally granted for the enclosure of the fields in question. Since then there do not appear to have been any further serious public disturbances over the issue.

In 1844 details of the Newbury force were published in the Police and Constabulary Lists, the forerunner of the modem day Police Almanac (*Appendix 7*). It will be noted that the population for the borough is now shown as being 6,500 and the force uniform is described as being blue, with white embroidery and buttons.

In the 19th century, before the use of telephones, the only means of communication with other Police Forces was either by a personal visit (rarely done unless the journey was comparatively local) or by letter. When it was considered necessary to circulate details of wanted persons, lists of stolen and found property, etc., the originating force would write to the Commissioner of the Metropolis, who was also responsible, under the jurisdiction of the Home Office, for publishing and circulating the Police Gazette (still referred to by some older authorities at this time as the 'Hue and Cry'). This publication was sent to all forces within the United Kingdom at frequent intervals. In the Police Gazette dated Friday, 6 September, 1844 there is an entry originating from Newbury which deals with a horse which had been found locally and thought to have been stolen. The entry reads as follows:

'Detained at Newbury, Berks, supposed to have been stolen, a black mare, 14 hands 2 inches high, star on the forehead, some girth marks on the ribs of both sides,

switch tail, has had one or more colts, has two white marks on the nearside of the poll, long in the waist, and rather low in the back - Information to be given to Thomas Price, Yeoman of Speen, or to Alfred Milsom, Chief Constable of New bury.

There was a general increase in the number of prisoners awaiting trial at the Borough Quarter Sessions and in July 1842 the number stood at sixteen, a somewhat different situation from the position a few years earlier when it was recorded that there were just two prisoners for the half year. During this time the Watch Committee agreed to reimburse the Chief Constable the sum of 2/6d for the hire of a sedan chair to transport a witness to court to give evidence on behalf of the prosecution in a case of aggravated assault, by order of the Magistrates. The records also show a rather curious payment of 3/- being made to Henry Beck, the day constable, for the purchase of fireworks. It is perhaps possible that these were going to be used at some sort of official gala arranged by the council, but there is no further explanation given in the records.

The years 1843 and 1844 passed without any major incidents, but the prisoner numbers appear to have remained fairly constant, as it was recorded that there was a total of thirteen cases awaiting trial at the Epiphany Quarter Sessions, in 1844;. This same year an outbreak of smallpox occurred at Abingdon Jail which required a re-adjustment of the local jail population. There is also reference in the minutes to a heavy bill of £22. 10. 6d. to be paid by the Borough in respect of a case at the County Assizes (which would have been held at Abingdon at that time) to one Jane Smith . No further details of either the nature or cause of the excess costs are recorded. The amount of fines received for summary convictions throughout the year of 1844 was shown as being £144. Ss. 4d. It was also recorded that Superintendent Deane had been paid the sum of 6s. 9d. for a journey to Hungerford to apprehend and convey two prisoners back to Newbury; Thomas and George Dell were subsequently charged with assaulting Officer Beck. Throughout 1844 there was much mention in the Watch Committee minutes of a large bill having been received from Messrs. Colley, Smith & Co. which appears to have been 'laid on the table' for sometime awaiting a decision as to how it should be paid. It was eventually agreed that it should be paid off at the rate of £50 per quarter so as to ease the cost to the ratepayer. There are no details of this case, but it appears to be something that had gone against the authorities in some form or another.

In November 1845 another officer fell foul of the discipline procedure, as it was reported that the Mayor had suspended Joseph Allen, one of the original Night Patrolmen for misconduct and prevarication and had appointed a J.King in his place. This action was supported and agreed upon by the whole of the Watch Committee.

Throughout this period there is frequent mention within the records of payments made for the services of Special Constables, who appear to have been used to supplement the regular officers at the time of the 'Hiring Fairs' and other times of potential disorder, such as the dispute over the enclosure issue. One of the duties of the Chief Constable under the direction of the Borough Treasurer was the collection of outstanding rates, market tolls, fees, etc. In the early years of the force 's existence it was reported that the Church Wardens and Overseers were greatly in arrears of their watch rate payments, and it was ordered on one occasion that if these rates were not paid within 14 days, proceedings were to be instituted. As they were still in arrears some two months later, the Chief Constable was ordered to take proceedings to clear the arrears. This issue could well have been the cause of the special enquiry that was held as a result of Dr. Binny challenging the authorities regarding the rating issue *(see Chapter 3 pages 23 & 24)*.

In 1845 preparations were in hand to enlarge the Borough, so the work of the small force would undoubtedly increase. In general the first ten years of the force 's existence passed fairly well with just the occasional minor hiccup.

CHAPTER FIVE
1846 - 1855 THE EARLY MIDDLE YEARS
DEATH OF THE FIRST CHIEF CONSTABLE
DEATH OF TWO JAILERS
RIOT AT MANSION HOUSE DURING PARLIAMENTARY ELECTIONS

The year 1846 appears to have passed without any sort of major incident involving the Police. In April, 1847 Officers John Tompkins and Edward Wilder resigned and their places were taken by James Wyatt, a shoemaker aged 30 years, and Henry Wait, aged 37 years, also described as a shoemaker. During this particular month the council drafted various by-laws for the good rule of the Borough, including one forbidding the use of dog carts within Borough limits and another imposing a penalty of £2 for conduct likely to cause a breach of the peace. There were a number of others, including one for exhibiting and distributing profane, indecent and offensive material. One assumes that the local law enforcement authorities, in the shape of the new police, must have encountered problems with such behaviour for the council to consider it necessary to bring in a by-law to cover it. Also included in the list were some basic by-laws to cover the general nuisance type of problems that exist in any society, such as throwing stones to the annoyance of residents or passengers, making slides in the snow, causing danger to passengers and residents, etc., and a general one for the better regulation of the town market regarding the sale of grain and seeds. In accordance with the law these draft by-laws were sent to the Home Secretary for his approval. It was subsequently recorded at a Watch Committee Meeting held on 6 May, 1847 that the Secretary of State for the Home Office, Sir George Grey, had replied to the council requesting further information on the proposed by-law referring to dog carts as he wanted to know the nature of the inconvenience caused by the use of such carts. He also considered that the proposed by-law for conduct likely to cause a breach of the peace was too general and unsuitable for the circumstances of the Borough of Newbury; he recommended that it should be omitted. In order to obtain direct evidence in respect of the proposed 'Dog Cart' by-law, the Watch Committee directed Constable Henry Beck to provide evidence to substantiate the application. The officer informed the committee that he had received complaints from several gentlemen in carriages and from general inhabitants of the serious inconvenience and great nuisance occasioned by the use of dogs drawing carts. The Rector of the Parish appears to have been one of the principle complainants. One of the main causes of complaint in respect of these small dog-drawn carts was that coachmen and drivers of large carts and wagons had difficulty spotting these small vehicles from their lofty seating positions, exacerbated by their habit of trotting haphazardly in the street. The Chief Constable, Alfred Milsom, also gave evidence before the Watch Committee in support of this issue, stating that he too had received several complaints and had witnessed the great inconvenience and annoyance caused to inhabitants by the dog carts. Itinerant pedlars appear to have been the main users of dog-drawn carts. As a result of these submissions the Town Clerk was requested to procure minutes of the evidence obtained and reply to the Secretary of State accordingly. As to the second proposed by-law relating to conduct likely to cause a breach of the peace, it was resolved to abandon it on the recommendations of the Secretary of State.

It is of interest to note that the Watch Committee sought a by-law to cover disorderly behaviour causing a possible breach of the peace, as it clearly suggests that such conduct was a problem within the Borough It was obviously preferable to have a specific Act to deal with this nuisance rather than a general charge against the common law, and, although the Secretary of State would not agree to the issue of such a by-law, it does not deflect from the fact that the Watch Committee was far-sighted in trying to obtain a positive piece of legislation to cover unruly behaviour. Even in fairly recent times there has been a distinct lack of direct legislation covering this type of offence. The remaining by-laws, after various amendments and further clarification, came into being in August, 1847.

At a Watch Committee Meeting held on 7 July, 1847 it was agreed to appoint a Mr. John Whiting as a Night Patrol Officer in place of George Noyes, who had become disabled. (The records show no prior mention of Noyes and it is not known when he was originally appointed.) Interestingly, during the course of this year, the Watch Committee decided to stop the provision of refreshments to officers on duty on 5th November and the Michaelmas Fair dates. From then on they were expected to provide their own food for these extended hours of duty. It also suggests that these two annual events were fairly lively occasions requiring the continuous presence of officers. In the light of the railway being in full operation, it was also mentioned at the same meeting that there would have to be a revamp of the expenses paid to the Jailer in conveying prisoners to Reading. In February 1848 the council submitted a petition to Parliament requesting the repeal of the Window Tax.

At a Watch Committee meeting held on 3rd January, 1849 it was agreed that two extra Night Patrol Officers (Watchmen) be appointed for a limited period only. It was also agreed that they should commence their duties at 11 pm and continue until the day officers came on duty, and this arrangement was to last until the first week in March; proper clothing was to be provided and returned at the expiration of their limited contract. The records do not identify these two men but they were subsequently discharged, as agreed, on 7 April, 1849. For the council to take this action involving additional expenditure, one can but surmise that there was some cause for concern regarding cover by the existing 'night watch'.

At the first meeting of the Watch Committee on 3 January 1850 it was reported that the jailer, Thomas Samuels, had died, and that one Henry Bradley had been appointed in his place; unfortunately Mr. Bradley also died in early 1851 and a Mr. James Frewin was appointed jailer in his place.

In November, 1850 the Watch Committee again decided to employ temporary Night Patrol Officers for the winter months, their terms of employment to expire on I st March, 185 I, and the records show that the two men appointed were William Langton and William North. Whether or not it was the same William Langton who was dismissed in 1840 for stealing straw is not known, but it does appear to be a possibility, as he was obviously an experienced officer having previously been in command of the night section. The fact that the original charge of straw stealing appears to have been a fairly minor affair, it is credible that the council took him on in a lower capacity. However, it is just a speculation on a possibility. These two could well have been those employed during the previous winter months.

In February 1852, as a result of various regular officers being required to attend the Assizes at Reading for an extended period, the Watch committee swore in three additional constables, Messrs. Thomas Warner, Hugh Gauntlett and Thomas Langton, on a temporary basis. This seems to suggest that the regular officers were involved in fairly substantial cases during this period as only the more serious offences were tried at the County Assizes.

The Chief Constable, Alfred Milsom, passed away on 22 May, 1852 and his death appears to have been very sudden and unexpected. As a result of this a full meeting of the Borough Council was held on 7 July, 1852 and it was decided to appoint Mr. George Deane, the Night Superintendent, as general superintendent of the whole force in place of the deceased Alfred Milsom, and instead of using the title Chief Constable, in future the senior officer in charge of the Borough Force would be known as Superintendent. (This arrangement was in keeping with a number of the smaller Borough Forces in describing the rank of the Chief Officer). It was also decided that his hours of duty would be from 9 am to 10 pm daily and that, in addition to his present salary, he would have the privileges arising from the day summonses and warrants. (It was the practice of the Court at this time to pay a standard fee for the service and execution of such documents.) It was also decided to appoint a sergeant who would be in charge of the Night Section, and his hours of duty would be from 10 pm to 7.30 am the following morning. His wages were to be 15 shillings per week with the additional privileges arising from the night summonses. It will be noted that from now on the rank structure of the force had changed slightly in respect of the titles of the two senior officers; the officer in charge of the Force as a whole was now called 'Superintendent' and his second-in-command was a sergeant. The sergeant's insignia, certainly in the latter years of the Force's existence, was three chevrons with a crown above.

The Council subsequently appointed John Hill as Sergeant to commence his duties within this appointment as from 10 July, 1852 at a wage of 15 shillings per week plus privileges arising from the night summonses, etc. Sergeant Hill 's background is not mentioned in the records, but by this time the normal process for selecting the more senior ranks suggests that he would have had some previous experience in another force prior to his appointment at Newbury.

On Monday, 19 July, 1852 polling in Newbury for the Parliamentary Elections, commenced and soon disintegrated into violence, which resulted in the 'Riot Act' being read to the mob, which, even for the 19th century, was a fairly rare occurrence. It is reported that polling commenced at 9 am on the first day (polling appears to have lasted for two days) and it appeared to create a great deal of interest. At about 10 am a large number of supporters of the various candidates arrived in the town bearing their favours and, as they drove through Northbrook Street, they were greeted with shouts of "free trade" from what is described as 'a motley group of men carrying loaves of bread on poles'. However, nothing of a serious nature occurred at this time. The first real sign of trouble took place at around 2 pm when a local gentleman, a certain Captain Willes of Hungerford, was passing the Mansion House and a man described in contemporary reports as being a 'ruffianly fellow', approached him and dealt the captain several blows on the head with a long pole, knocking off his hat. The good captain does not appear to have sustained any serious injury and, seeing that he was somewhat outnumbered, replaced his hat and good humouredly passed on his way. His assailant was instantly arrested by the Police and locked up.

There then followed an occurrence which was obviously the subject of much debate over the ensuing weeks, for it is reported that the Mayor liberated the prisoner, an action which appears to have given great offence to the friends of the Conservative candidates. (On the face of things it appears rather strange that the Mayor intervened in this manner, however as Mayor, he was also a Magistrate and he no doubt dealt with the prisoner in accordance with the evidence he had to hand, a fact borne out by the comments he made in his letter to the press the following week). At the time his actions certainly appear to have caused something of a sensation within the Borough, as he considered it necessary to have an open letter published in the Reading Mercury the following week outlining the reason for his actions. (A copy of this letter is shown in full at Appendix 8).

Later the same evening it is reported that several skirmishes between some voters and the mob took place at Speenhamland. The following day the polls opened at 8 am and it is reported that much of the interest had abated. At 11 am Mr. Dyne, a builder, was seen to be riding his horse at the head of a group of his workmen, who were all carrying sticks. The whole procession was accompanied by music as it paraded through the main streets of the town, and a large crowd fell in behind the procession. On reaching the top of Bartholomew Street near the Mansion House, the Mayor, Mr. William Dredge, informed Mr. Dyne that he was acting very injudiciously, and that if a Breach of the Peace should take place he would be held fully responsible. There is no clear information as to what happened immediately after the Mayor's intervention; one suspects that the crowd just hung around the town centre. Then, at 2.30 pm it is reported that the mob approached the eastern entrance to the Mansion House, overpowered the Police on duty there, forced open the gates, entered the building and commenced destroying the actual polling booths. The clerks were obliged to make a judicious retreat with the Polling books and general paperwork. The mob then turned its attention to the Sheriffs Deputy, Mr. Beckhuson, striking at him repeatedly with their long poles. At that moment the Mayor once again appeared quickly on the scene and his presence stopped any further attacks upon the hapless Sheriff's Deputy. Some sort of order was restored and the polls were allowed to continue until the close. A number of voters inside the Polling Station at the time were roughly handled by the mob, although no serious injuries appear to have been sustained.

The Borough Magistrates must have realised that the general situation was ripe for further trouble, and hastily convened a meeting at 3 pm for the sole purposes of discussing the public order situation and considering the swearing in of additional special constables. However, before taking this action, they sent out various members of the Borough Police Force to ascertain the general state of the town. Subsequent reports received from the officers suggested that the general situation had calmed down, and there were no signs of any disturbances within the borough. In the light of this information it was decided that there was no necessity to swear in additional Special Constables at this time, but as a safeguard the Magistrates ordered that all regular officers should remain on duty until further notice.

By 5 pm it became obvious that the situation had once again deteriorated and the crowd was reassembling around the Mansion House. The magistrates decided to play safe and swore in large numbers of special constables. One contemporary report suggests that this hurried swearing-in resulted in a failure to issue all the special constables with normal truncheons, etc., and therefore some were forced to arm themselves with whatever weapons they could lay their hands on, legs of tables or anything resembling a truncheon. The two men who appeared to take command of this hastily mustered force were Messrs. Shaw and Martin, both of whom were Borough Councillors, and had had past experience serving on the Watch Committee.

By 7 pm the crowd had grown dramatically and the situation deteriorated when the mob crowded around the Mansion House began to act in a disorderly and riotous manner. At 8 pm it was decided that it was necessary to read the Riot Act, and this was done by the Town Clerk. Once again the Mayor, William Dredge, appears to have been well to the forefront in trying to calm down the situation, as it is recorded that he used every exertion in his power to try to get the crowd to disperse, but to no avail.

As the crowd did not disperse as required, in accordance with the reading of the Riot Act, the Police, with the aid of the Specials, started to make arrests, and in total some seventeen men were arrested. The judicial system was speedier than we have come to expect today, as all the arrested men remained in custody overnight and subsequently appeared before the Borough Magistrates the following morning. They were charged with various offences such as riotous and disorderly conduct, assault on Police, general drunkenness, failing to disperse, etc. A total of eleven were convicted and sentenced to various short terms of imprisonment with hard labour varying from four months to two weeks. One prisoner, who was just charged with failure to leave the scene after the Riot Act had been read, was discharged with a general warning, and the remaining five prisoners, against whom no charges were preferred, were discharged.

Contemporary reports speak highly of the actions of the Specials and they were congratulated on the laudable manner in which they carried out their duties, ' Saving their neighbours from the hands of the ruffianly mob'. The same report also made mention of the Police Officers of the Borough, who it was claimed discharged their duties most satisfactorily, and were entitled to the thanks of the inhabitants for their efficient services.

As a footnote to the election disturbances, it will be recalled that Captain

George Willes of Hungerford, who was himself a County Magistrate, was assaulted on the first day of the election and an alleged offender was taken into custody immediately following this incident. The affair caused a fair amount of controversy when the prisoner was later released on the Mayor's orders. Captain Willes subsequently summoned Frederick Bradley for assault and the case was heard before the Borough Magistrates on Monday, 2 August, 1852. This case appears to have caused a great deal of local interest and took up most of the day. Finally however, the Magistrates dismissed the case when the identity of his assailant could not be fully proved although they fully accepted that an assault had certainly taken place upon Captain Willes. So ended the final case arising from the disorderly behaviour at the election.

Although not specifically mentioned, one gets the impression that the Mayor, William Dredge, is certainly deserved commendation as he appeared to be in the forefront on the side of law and order throughout the whole period, and he comes across as being the main driving force.

In 1852, the Watch Committee found it necessary to purchase a new Charge Book at a cost of £ I. 10s. 0d., perhaps an indication of a fairly steady flow of prisoners passing through the system.

Later in the year William Buckeridge was appointed as a Night Patrol Officer. (The records are a little confusing at this point, as they state that this appointment was in respect of Noyes, although an earlier entry stated that Whiting had been Noye 's replacement.)

On 5 September, 1853 a joint written request was received from the night section officers requesting an increase in wages, and was subsequently referred to the full Borough Council with a recommendation that the Sergeant's pay should be increased from 15 shillings to £1 per week and that the pay of the rest of the night patrolmen be increased from I 2 shillings to I 4 shillings per week, to commence from 24 September, I 853. This recommendation was adopted in full.

These pay rises appear to have prompted other personnel working in the law enforcement fraternity in Newbury to seek additional wages and the Jailer, Mr. Frewin, was given an increase of £5 per year plus an additional £4 per year for the loss of "certain privileges which he had previously enjoyed", although what exactly these comprised is not recorded. Superintendent Deane's wages were subsequently increased to £1. 5s. 0d. per week commencing on 4 December, 1855. There is no mention of Constable Beck receiving a wage increase at this time, but he had previously been given a rise in April, 1853, making his wages 12 shillings per week, plus expenses, so this might well have been considered sufficient.

Since the formation of the new type of Police Force created by the Municipal Corporations Act, 1835, there had been a certain amount of pressure applied by central government for amalgamations, especially with regard to the smaller Borough Forces. Generally the suggested amalgamations would have been with the local County Force, but the Berkshire County Force only came into existence in 1856, so there was no fear of Newbury losing its own force at this stage, whereas in other parts of the country County Forces were already established. The question of amalgamations was high on the central political agenda of 1854. Local records show that, at a full Borough Council meeting on 4 January 1854, a letter from the Mayor of Southampton was tabled together with a petition against a report from a Select Committee of the House of Commons which recommended that all small Boroughs should be consolidated with districts and counties for police purposes. It was agreed to support Southampton in opposing this motion. Some six months later on the 8th June, 1854 another special meeting of the Council was held to discuss the same sort of issue, regarding a further letter from the Lord Mayor of York, requesting the Mayor of Newbury to attend a meeting in London the following day with all the Borough Mayors of England and Wales who had their own Police Forces. The meeting would consider the subject of the Police Bill introduced by Lord Palmerston on the question of amalgamations. It was agreed at the special Council meeting that the Mayor should attend and offer resistance to any provisions affecting the privileges of the Borough and oppose any attempt at innovation of the current system of policing as it existed under the Municipal Act.

A further special meeting of the full council was held on 16 June, when the Mayor, Mr. J. F. Hickman, reported that he had attended the meeting of the Mayors held in London on 9 June, 1854 and that the outcome had been an agreement that all the Boroughs should resolutely oppose the Police Bill introduced by Lord Palmerston. A form of petition was accordingly submitted to (and approved by) the meeting and it was resolved that the Mayor be requested to affix the Corporation Seal to this document. It was also resolved that the petition be forwarded to Robert Palmer, Esq. M.P. and that the other County members be requested to support this petition. As most of the Boroughs managed to retain their own forces until many years later, it is assumed that the Palmerston Bill was not entirely successful in its ultimate aims. However, the question of amalgamations has been an on-going subject and, over the years, there have been large scale amalgamations with the majority of smaller Borough forces being swallowed up in the latter part of the 19th Century, and the majority of the medium sized boroughs losing their independent status in the large scale amalgamations of 194 7, after the Second World War. The next round of amalgamations came in 1968, when larger Boroughs were merged with the surrounding forces .

Even today there is talk of creating still larger police units into groupings covering bigger areas - it is an ongoing theme. However, going back to 1854 this was a period when there was much debate in Parliament about the system of policing and of making it compulsory for all counties to provide a proper paid Police Force for their respective areas. This eventually came about a few years later through the introduction of the County and Borough Police Act, 1856. The Crimea War was still being fought in 1854 resulting in large numbers of additional men joining the colours and, following the normal practice of the British Army at this time, at the end of such a conflict, demobbed soldiers were discharged somewhat haphazardly on to the overstretched home labour market. Unable to be absorbed by the labour market, some men turned to less lawful pursuits, just as they had during the early years of the century at the end of the Napoleonic Wars.

One can appreciate that, notwithstanding all the other factors, this particular issue could well have helped politicians to focus their minds more closely on policing issues of the day. Another factor was that prior to 1856 legislation had allowed counties voluntarily to form their own paid Police Forces. A number of counties throughout the country had done so and, because this had proved successful, it was the Government's intention to bring all counties into line by making it compulsory for them to have their own professional Police Forces through the introduction of the 1856 Act.

However, we are now getting a little in advance of ourselves, as these events are still in the future. In 1855 there was a change in the law which allowed cases of petty larceny to be tried at the local Magistrates' Court instead of having to be heard at the higher Quarter Sessions Court.

Also in 1855 it is recorded that Superintendent Deane was paid the additional sum of 15 shillings in expenses for collecting a dead 'mad' dog from Lambourn. The records do not elaborate further on this issue, and in view of the fact that Lambourn was well outside the jurisdiction of the Borough one can only assume that 'the dog may have died from rabies and that the authorities wanted the carcass to be removed or examined. The task would have fallen to the nearest professional Police Force, in this case Newbury, as the Berkshire County Force was still not in being.

The Newbury Force had been in existence for nearly 20 years and for all intents and purposes was ticking along fairly well, and on the face of things at least it appeared to be an efficient, well run small force.

The year 1856 was a memorable one for law enforcement, for this was the year which saw the formation of the Berkshire County Constabulary and other county forces throughout the United Kingdom. By 29 March the newly appointed Chief Constable of Berkshire, Colonel Fraser, had divided the County into six territorial divisions and one Headquarters. These divisions or districts were as follows:

CHAPTER SIX

THE THIRD DECADE ~ 1856 - 1865
FORMATION OF THE BERKS COUNTY POLICE FORCE
NEWBURY SUPERINTENDENT ENLARGES HIS AREA OF RESPONSIBILITY
APPOINTMENT OF A NEW SERGEANT
OUTBREAK OF CATTLE PLAGUE IN THE BOROUGH

The year 1856 was a memorable one for law enforcement, for this was the year which saw the formation of the Berkshire County Constabulary and other county forces throughout the United Kingdom. By 29 March the newly appointed Chief Constable of Berkshire, Colonel Fraser, had divided the County into six territorial divisions and one Headquarters. These divisions or districts were as follows:

- Central District, based on Reading and the surrounding area
- Reading Borough was already being policed by its own Borough Force
- South Western District, based at Newbury, covered the surrounding parishes
- Newbury Borough still operated its own force.
- Eastern District based at Windsor covered the surrounding area -Windsor had its own Borough Force for the town
- Western District based at Wantage, covered Wantage and the surrounding area. - Wantage, which had previously had its own force, amalgamated with the newly formed County Force
- Northern District based at Abingdon covered the surrounding area- here again, Abingdon still had its own Force for the town
- Finally the North Western District based at Faringdon Each district / division was under the command of a superintendent.

The immediate area of interest as far as this book is concerned is the South Western District with its divisional headquarters at Newbury. The officer in charge was Superintendent George Dowde and he was assisted by two Sergeants, William Harfield who was based at East Ilsley and Sergeant John Barnes who was stationed at Hungerford. Constables were stationed at Aldermaston,

Thatcham, Crookham, Kintbury, Enborne Street, Inkpen, Shefford, Boxford, Chapel Bucklebury, Chieveley, Wickham, Hampstead Norreys, Peasemore, Newbury (3), East Ilsley and Chaddleworth. The imposition upon the county of such a large organisation produced difficulties in accommodating all the officers resulting in some inevitable 'chopping and changing' within the early months of the force 's existence; this, however, was the original basic structure.

The new County Police Station for the South Western District was eventually sited in Pelican Lane, (known then as Pelican Road) Newbury and, although the Station was well within the Borough area, its jurisdiction stretched beyond the Borough limits. The Newbury Borough Force remained responsible for law enforcement issues within the Borough. Past local historians have perhaps found it difficult to separate the jurisdiction of the two local forces: some written accounts give the impression that the County Force took over law enforcement issues in the Borough from its inception, but this was certainly not the case and only came about some 19 years later in 1875.

With the Government's introduction of the Police Act of 1856, which compelled all counties which had, as yet, not voluntarily formed their own forces, to do so as soon as possible. It was also at this time that central Government took on indirect responsibility for all Forces, both new and old, including the Borough and County Forces which were already in existence. This was done by paying a grant of 25% towards the cost of each Force. (This grant was increased in the mid-1870s.) In order to ensure uniformity and general efficiency, along with this new Act the Government also introduced inspectors who were required to visit all Forces annually and to report their findings direct to the Home Office. For example, if a Force was considered to be inefficient the Government could, in theory at least, withhold the grant. This system still applies to this day. A copy of a Home Office letter certifying the efficiency of the Newbury Force is shown in Appendix 9.

The year 1856 saw the retirement, due to ill health, of the Jailer of the Borough Jail, Mr. Frewin: George Deane, the Superintendent in charge of the Borough Force, replaced him. This appointment suggests that Mr. Deane was enlarging not only his field of civic responsibility, but also his salary. His wife was eventually appointed Matron to the jail at a retaining salary of £3 .10.0d per year, but whether or not she was paid additional sums when called upon to perform this duty is not known. One of the conditions of Mr. Deane's new appointment was that he should reside at the same premises as the previous jailer, either at the jail or at the old workhouse which was situated next door. Mr. Deane was seemingly a fairly busy man as his hours of duty as the senior Borough Police Officer were 9 am to 10 pm daily, with no days off. He obviously had very little time for himself, but he appears to have combined his jailer duties with his police role fairly successfully.

In April 1857 the Council received a request from Mrs. Frewin, the wife of the previous jailer and herself the ex-matron, asking for financial assistance, but it was decided that the Council could not assist directly with this request. At the same meeting Mr. Thomas Fidler sought permission from the Watch Committee to use the large room at the Borough Jail for Divine Services, permission was given, but only on Sundays. It was obviously felt that the prisoners ' spiritual needs were important.

On 20 June 1857 the Watch Committee suspended Constable Stephen Justice on 'no pay' for an undisclosed misdemeanour. However, it could not have been a very serious matter for he was fully reinstated on 8 July.

The Government Inspector's report for 1857 makes for interesting reading as it gives good background information on the general Force ' set-up ' which existed at the time. The report reads as follows:

'The Police Force of Newbury, when inspected in April, consisted of one superintendent and one constable for day duty, and one Sergeant and jour Constables for night duty, and it was stated that two additional supernumerary Constables were also employed for night duty during the winter months.

The organisation of the Police Force was however not of a satisfactory character, as the Superintendent and one Constable only received proper uniform clothing, and were required to devote their whole time to the Police service; the Sergeant and the four night Constables were in the daytime allowed to follow their own trades as masons and labourers, and received only in the way of clothing a great coat and hat.

The Watch Committee on the 8" June re-organised the Force, which is now composed of one Superintendent, one Sergeant and five Constables who are supplied with proper uniform clothing, and required to devote their whole time in the service of the Police.

Another Constable is also appointed to assist in day duty, but he also holds the appointment of Bellman and Town Crier.

Some alterations were required in the cells, and I was informed that these matters should receive early attention.

I consider that the duties are now satisfactorily provided for, and that the whole Police Force is in an efficient state in regard to numbers and organisation.

The area of the Borough comprises of 1,722 acres, and the population in 1851 amounted to 6,574 persons.'

As stated in the inspector's report, the Watch Committee acted positively on all the suggestions made and, at the same time, also reviewed their appointments procedure in respect of potential officers. This precluded the selection of officers under 30 or over 40 years of age. (It will be noted from the following pages that the Watch Committee did not always adhere to this policy.)

At a special meeting of the Borough Watch Committee held on 14 August 1857 it was reported that a number of applications had been received for the post of Sergeant, which suggests that, for reasons unknown, Sergeant Hill had left the force. The only possible clue to his retirement could be that at Newbury Borough Quarter Sessions on 2 November a man by the name of Oliver Cromwell was charged with wounding Sergeant Hill in the execution of his duty. Cromwell was subsequently sentenced to one month's hard labour in the House of Correction at Reading for this assault. The two main applicants for the vacant post were Mr. Lewis Dorl, aged 24 years, and John Lee, aged 30 years. Dorl appears to have been well under the recommended age for appointment according to the Government Inspector's comments in the earlier communication. However, Lee was the successful candidate and was appointed to the vacant post of Sergeant, subject to him producing satisfactory testimonials, birth certificate, etc. and on his leaving the newly formed Berkshire County Force. Lee was in fact Pc 28 in the Berkshire Constabulary, having also previously served in the Metropolitan Police for some 17 months. For reasons not explained, he appears to have resigned from the County Force at this time, so either he did not pursue this appointment or the committee had a change of heart about him, because he was not appointed. A possible reason could be that on I June, 1857, whilst serving in the Berkshire Constabulary, he was the subject of two discipline offences and was fined five shillings for absenting himself from his station without leave, and being under the influence of liquor. These types of discipline offences were not unusual and drink was a common factor in those days. It must have been a hard life for the officers who had to work a seven day week with little or no time for relaxation.

As a result of this abortive appointment a further special meeting was held by the Watch Committee on 11 September, 1857 when a short list of three applicants was produced for the post of Sergeant. The list included Henry Reading from Reading, John Bull from Greenham and John William Rose, aged 38 years from Bermondsey, London. Subject to a satisfactory character reference from the Metropolitan Police, Rose was the selected candidate. At the interview Rose informed the panel that he was currently working in the salt trade but had previously served as a constable in the Metropolitan Police from 1849 to 1852, leaving the force in consequence of a wrong identification when dealing with two brothers and taking the wrong man into custody. He claimed that he had therefore resigned his office to prevent an action being brought against him for false imprisonment. However, the testimonials he produced at the time of the interview appeared to be entirely satisfactory. A subsequent check was made with the Metropolitan Police, regarding his background details whilst employed as a Police Officer within that force, and whether or not it was the result of this check or for an entirely different reason one cannot say, but Sergeant Rose's appointment in the Newbury Borough Force must quality as the shortest on record as it lasted just three nights. A special meeting of the

Watch Committee was convened on 30 September, 1857, specifically to receive a report that Sergeant Rose had been suspended by the Mayor the previous evening for misconduct and the committee agreed to sack the unfortunate Rose forthwith. It was not stated exactly what the 'misconduct' was, but one can assume it was something of a serious nature for such drastic action to be taken so soon after making the appointment. An opinion was expressed by one of the councillors that the Sergeant was entirely unfit for his office.

As a result of Rose's dismissal, a further meeting of the Watch Committee was held on 14 October in order to appoint his successor and on this occasion there were three applicants for the post, Thomas Hinds, Lewis Dorl (again) and David Dredge. Hinds was the successful candidate and he subsequently took up his duties as Sergeant on 21 October, 1857. Hinds was aged 25 years, a married man with two children. Until the time of his appointment he had been a serving officer, Pc 12 in the newly formed Berkshire County Constabulary and a Constable in the Metropolitan Police before that. He had earlier been employed on the railway.

The Watch Committee appears to have acted upon all the recommendations made by the Government Inspector in his 1857 Report, for his 1858 Report noted that the whole Force had been reorganised, that the station house had been remodelled and a new office had been erected. The Report also stated that the cells had been improved to a satisfactory standard making them suitable for the detention of prisoners, and commented that duties appeared to be well arranged and the requirements of the Borough satisfactorily provided for. The Inspector considered it an efficient and disciplined Force.

During the next few years everything appeared to run fairly smoothly with just the more mundane issues recorded, such as the purchase of drags for use on the canal and river, at a cost of £2.5s.0d. This purchase perhaps suggests that it was not uncommon for the Police to be called upon to retrieve bodies, etc., from the various waterways within the Borough. Another minute records the fact that Superintendent Deane objected to the use of the large room at the Jail / Workhouse for services and the arrangement previously agreed appears now to have been dropped. There is also mention of the fact that a greater number of prisoners were being processed through the system in recent years, especially during 1859, and comment is made that it was a lot cheaper to have them dealt with before the Magistrates than a higher court. (Things do not change much as this argument is frequently put forward today.) The increase in prisoner turnover suggests that the Force was fairly active, but the down side to this increase in arrests was the extra cost of prosecutions which the Council had to bear.

In 1859 the Government Inspector of the day, a Captain Willis, found the Police establishment at Newbury to be efficient but passed comment on the poor quality of the officers' greatcoats. As a result of this criticism the Watch Committee arranged for all the officers to attend one of their meetings and produce their greatcoats, whereupon it was generally agreed that the coats were of a poor quality and arrangements were made to purchase new ones for the entire force at a cost of £3 .16s.0d. for the Superintendent's coat and a total of £12. 5s. 0d for all the remaining rank and file. It is interesting to note that there is a mention in the Minutes to the effect that the council had been ' pennywise and pound foolish' when they purchased the coats in the first place, as they were definitely of an inferior quality.

The number of prisoners going through the judicial system remained fairly high throughout 1860 and 1861 and once again the financial issue was raised. At a meeting in 1860 it was reported that John Hill had been appointed Gas Meter Inspector for the Borough - could this have been the ex-Sergeant who retired in 1857? At a full Council meeting on 9 November 1860 it was decided to change the formation of the various Council Committees so that one-third of the members sat on the Watch Committee, one third on the Finance Committee and one-third on the Estates Committee, the mayor to sit on all Committees.

Throughout this whole period the records show that regular payments were made for the use of Special Constables, suggesting that their services were often required. In addition to his many other duties, Superintendent Deane was also the officer in charge of the Borough Fire Brigade. (This was a common practice throughout the country at this time, and in some places this arrangement of Police / Fire Brigades carried on well in to the twentieth century, right up to the

Second World War).

In 1860 the force implemented a far-sighted Pension Scheme for its serving Officers whereby 2½% of their weekly wage was deducted and placed in the Superannuation Fund. This fund was also 'topped up ' from revenue acquired from fines and fees.

During the latter part of 1860 a question was raised within the Council regarding the collection of fines and fees, for which Superintendent Deane gained a small additional income. It was subsequently established that the Superintendent received an average of about 7/2d. per week in addition to his basic salary for carrying out extraneous jobs such as serving summonses, executing warrants, collecting fines and fees, distributing notices to licensed victuallers, conveyance of prisoners, etc. It was eventually decided by the Borough Council that, with effect from I December 1860, this additional income would be replaced by an increase in his basic salary making it up to £1. 11s. 6d. per week. He would still receive a retaining fee of £2 per year for his attendance on the fire engine and the money he received from the Board of Guardians.

In March 1861 Pc. Kimber passed away having been off sick for some time, and an un-named supernumerary officer was taken on in his place.

In 1862 further discussion took place within the Council regarding the state of the Borough's fire appliances, and after the Councillors had inspected the machines it was declared that they were comparatively valueless in cases of fire fighting. It was decided that it had become an absolute necessity to obtain a more powerful engine and a more reliable and powerful water source. The meeting then discussed the possibility of having pipes laid under the streets from the Town Mill Head, but no final decision was made at this time on the water supply question.

Also around this time tenders were submitted for the provision of new hats and boots for the Force, and it was subsequently agreed to place an order with a local supplier for new hats, priced at 11 shillings each, and boots at 17 shillings per pair. One would imagine that at this time members of the Force were still wearing the tall ' stovepipe' reinforced top hats. The clothing issued to the various members of the Force at this time was as follows:-

- <u>Superintendent:</u> One dress coat, one hat, two pairs of trousers, two pairs of boots.
- <u>Sergeant:</u> One dress coat, one hat, two pairs of trousers, two pairs of boots, one great coat, one armlet.
- <u>Constables (5):</u> Dress coats, one hat, two pairs of trousers, two pairs of boots, greatcoat and armlet.
- <u>Constable / Bell man:</u> Dress coat, one hat, one pair of trousers, one pair of boots and one greatcoat.

At a meeting of the Watch Committee held on 7 October, 1862, two temporary night patrol officers, George Paulin and Charles Deane, were appointed to the force in place of Sergeant Hinds and Pc Justice, who were both on long term sick leave.

A Watch Committee meeting held on 20 November, 1863 agreed that the 'Night Watch Beat' would be extended no further westward than Andover Terrace on the Wash Road and not beyond Mr. Winsor's house on the Enborne Road. On the Newtown Road the limit of the beat was the new Union Workhouse. It was then agreed that all properties beyond those limits would be exempted from payments of the 'Watch Rates' but that all other properties within the Borough be deemed liable for payment of the rate. At the same meeting far reaching proposals were submitted for consideration regarding Borough Officers ' duty hours and methods of patrolling the various beats (*see Appendix 10 for full details*). It is difficult to conceive how the officers managed to survive the rigorous working hours required of them at this time. There were no fixed rest days and day officers worked 'split' tours covering morning, afternoon and evening hours. Night duty officers appear to have fared rather better in that they worked a ' straight ' shift.

In November 1863 the Council received a letter from Colonel Blandy, Chief Constable of the County Force, who suggested that the Borough Force use the same sort of forms, charge books, etc. as the county force and this was subsequently agreed upon. This was a good, practical idea that certainly would have simplified working arrangements at grass-roots levels. Col. Blandy probably wrote similar letters to all the Borough Forces within the County.

In February 1864 a further night patrol officer named Dibley was appointed on a short term basis, no further details are recorded.

Superintendent Deane was criticised by the Watch Committee on 12 January 1864 for not making proper returns to the Treasurer in respect of inquests and various licences. Also at this meeting the Treasurer asked for an additional salary to cover the extra work he was required to do in respect of the administration of the new Police Superannuation Fund. It was agreed to pay him an additional half guinea a quarter for this extra work.

On 12 July, 1864 it was reported that Pc Rosier had been ill and unable to perform any duties since 22 May. (This is the first mention in the records of this particular officer and so his date of appointment is unknown). It was also reported at the same meeting that Benny Lewis, having been appointed as a supernumerary in Pc. Rosier's place, had since been suspended. Acting on a report received from the Superintendent, the committee was of the opinion that he was not a fit and proper person to hold the office of Constable in the Newbury Borough Police Force. There is no further report on this situation. At an October meeting it was further reported that Pc Rosier was still on the 'sick list' but, to the committee's credit, they agreed to continue paying his salary. As this officer had been off duty since May one must assume he was a seriously sick man.

In December of 1864 the Watch Committee discussed a memorandum received from the Home Secretary relating to a national survey, which had been carried out earlier in the year, to determine the number of tramps and vagrants who were in the Borough on a certain night. It appears that the Newbury return had been completed incorrectly and the Home Secretary administered a mild rebuke and ordered that a new return be completed as soon as possible. The committee agreed that the original return was based on incorrect information, wrongly interpreted. The Home Secretary's memorandum reads as follows:-

'Mr. Waddington begs to acknowledge the receipt of the annual police return for the year ended 29 September last, and to request that the Head Constable will have the goodness to inform him of the cause of the extraordinary increase in the numbers of vagrants and tramps as shown in the present return, when compared with those given in the return for the previous year, being respectively for 1863, '41 ', and for

1864 '1679'. Mr. Waddington fears that some misunderstanding may have occurred as to the purport of the instructions under the head contained in the letter which accompanied the forms sent in July last, which were as follows, vis: 'With regard to vagrants and tramps, the rule adopted last year may again be followed for the present year, vis; that under this head should be included all vagrants who are known to the police as professional tramps, or as being without visible means of subsistence or any fixed place or residence and who may sleep within your borough on the night of the first Tuesday in the month of September, etc. etc.' It is thought probable that the total for the month may have been given in error, an early reply is requested.

Home Office, Whitehall, 61h December, 1864.'

The committee added a footnote to this entry which read:

'This return was made as assumed by Mr. Waddington under the misapprehension that the return was intended to be for 52 weeks, the actual total for the night in question was '43'' - just a slight drop from ' 1679'!

(Reproduced by kind permission of the Berkshire Record Office - N/AC 1/2/2)

In March 1865 it was considered necessary to have an additional Police Officer on duty on Market days from 10 am- 4 pm. This duty, it was agreed, would be split between two officers each working three hours every Thursday from 10 am to 1 pm and 1 pm to 4 pm respectively. Each man would be paid an extra shilling for the additional time involved. One assumes that they would have been required to perform some sort of split shifts, and that when they finished the Market duty they would have had the majority of their normal tour of duty to complete.

In July 1865 the Watch Committee discussed policing arrangements for the forthcoming elections and the fact that the Chief Constable of the Berkshire County Force, Colonel Blandy, had offered the services of County officers to assist in policing the elections within the Borough, if required. However, the Watch Committee declined the offer and decided that if any assistance was required it could be given by local Borough Special Constables.

The year 1865 was a memorable one as far as the general appearance of the Force was concerned. It was the year when the Borough Force, in common with numerous other Forces throughout the country, adopted the helmet-type headgear replacing the old 'stovepipe' top hats which had been worn since the force was formed. In a way this change-over was rather strange, as the original intention when the current Forces were first formed, had been to make the Officers look like ordinary citizens in uniform and to play down, as much as possible, the military look which it was considered the British general public associated with the continent, where police forces came under a centralised military style control and were, in fact, often part of the national standing army. Although the helmet is now always considered the traditional headgear of the British bobby, in fact it was originally a straight lift from the military, as most British infantry regiments were wearing this type of head-gear. We now find the Police deliberately adopting military style head-gear!

The year 1865 ended on a rather disturbing note. It was reported in December that the local cattle market had to be closed due to an outbreak of cattle plague, and it appears to have remained closed for some considerable time. There is no doubt that such an outbreak would have caused considerable additional work for the police force. There were also numerous reports of disturbances within the 'city area', generally considered the rougher part of the town, which would have kept the force fairly active.

CHAPTER SEVEN

1866-1870

DOUBLE MURDER~ BOROUGH ACQUIRES A NEW FIRE ENGINE~ PAY RISE
FOR THE FORCE~ FENIAN SCARE~ ENROLMENT OF ADDITIONAL SPECIALS
~SERGEANT'S LATE NIGHT DRINKING HABIT~ RESIGNATION AND
APPOINTMENT OF A NUMBER OF SERGEANTS IN QUICK SUCCESSION~
PUBLIC ORDER INCIDENT~ LICENSING ISSUES

The year 1866 started quietly enough but closed with a horrific double murder and suicide in December. The murders took place in a dwelling house situated in Eyles Buildings, Smith Crescent, Shaw; at this time this particular location was just outside the borough boundary; thus the case was dealt with by Superintendent Harfield of the Berkshire County Constabulary. In view of the evidence that the movements of the deceased parties (prior to their deaths) and those of their assailant on the night in question included a visit to a local Borough Public House, it would be safe to assume that members of the Borough Force were actively involved with the County Superintendent in subsequent investigations, and indeed, Sergeant Hinds of the Borough Force did give evidence at the inquests.

The brief facts of the case are as follows: the murderer, Henry Martin, had only just been released from Reading Prison where he had served a term of imprisonment for assault, prior to which he had been living with one of the victims, Eliza Shaw, in Eyles Buildings. Contemporary press reports suggest that Miss Shaw was a prostitute, and until the time of his arrest, Martin had been cohabiting with her. It appears that whilst Martin was a guest of Her Majesty, Eliza started to keep company with James Brett, who is described as being a 'Pot Boy' working at the 'Sun Beer House' in Clare Market Street, London, but residing at the time of the incident at the Eagle Public House, Bartholomew Street, Newbury. (The common name for this public house for some reason or other was the 'Hand and Heart'.) Following his release Martin obviously wanted to renew his association with Eliza and, on the night in question, he met with her and her new man in the 'Eagle' Public House. Contemporary reports show that a violent quarrel took place between the parties in the public house, after which both Brett and Eliza left and made their way to

Eliza's house at Shaw.

Various witnesses would later give evidence at the inquest suggesting that Martin was in a foul mood, and 'bent on mischief. He was heard to pass various remarks such as 'Revenge is sweet' and 'I'll not swing for them'. He also appeared to have made enquiries amongst the drinking fraternity for a hammer or a pickaxe, presumably to use to break in to Eliza's home. After leaving his drinking companions in the centre of Newbury, he made his way to Eliza's home, forced an entry and attacked both Brett and Eliza in their bed, using a knife and a butcher's cramp. The end result was a total ' blood-bath' with both victims sustaining horrific wounds, which proved fatal. Eliza appears to have died almost instantly, but Brett was still alive the following morning when Superintendent Harfield first arrived at the scene, but died a little later.

Subsequent enquiries suggested that some of the neighbours had been awoken by Eliza's screams but, as violent rows were not exactly uncommon in this household, no action was taken. The following morning a couple of the female neighbours felt sufficiently concerned to investigate and entered the house without going upstairs. Shortly afterwards Martin returned to the scene and apparently enquired of the neighbours whether or not they had heard any disturbance coming from Eliza's house during the preceding night. After he left, one of the neighbours who had previously visited the house became more suspicious and returned to make the horrific discovery. The Police were sent for and Superintendent Harfield of the County Force quickly arrived on the scene. Brett was still alive and a doctor was called, but he died of his injuries a short time later.

The Superintendent commenced his enquiries, and subsequently traced Martin's movements to the Crown Inn at West Mills, where it was established he had had a glass of beer and chatted with other customers prior to going along the canal towpath in the direction of Enborne. The Superintendent later found his body in the canal, his feet tied together with a handkerchief and his hat and boots neatly deposited on the towpath nearby.

At the inquest held on 6 December 1866 in respect of James Brett and Eliza Shaw, a verdict of 'wilful murder' was brought in against Martin. A second inquest then followed in respect of Martin, and a Verdict, a little strange to modern ears, was brought in that 'He wilfully murdered himself' - suicide in other words.

Back to the more mundane! It has previously been mentioned that in addition to his police duties, Superintendent Deane was in charge of the town's Fire Brigade. In 1866 there was mention in the council minutes of three other officials in the Brigade, Mr. Taylor, who is shown as being the Engineer, and two other officers, Sergeant G. Hayes and Corporal F. Stone. Additionally a total of 17 volunteer Firemen are shown in the records as 'privates' and all personnel appear to have been issued with distinctive uniforms.

It is also recorded that the Council had encountered some difficulties with Insurance Companies failing to pay promptly for services rendered by the Town Brigade, which suggests that, if the Brigade attended the scene of a fire where the premises were insured, a subsequent claim was made for this service by the Council against the appropriate Insurance Company. It was about this time that the Council was presented with a new fire engine, the donors being the Royal Exchange Insurance Company. Superintendent Deane is recorded as stating, that ' It was a first rate machine'. It is perhaps interesting to note that there is really nothing new in modern attempts to involve the private sector in sponsorship of some aspects of the services provided by local authorities. If the Royal Exchange insured a number of prominent premises within the Newbury area, it would have been to their advantage to ensure that the local Brigade had reasonable equipment. However, in this instance, one wonders whether Superintendent Deane was a little premature in 'singing the praises ' of the new machine as, at a council meeting later in the year, it was reported that the engine and hoses needed urgent attention costing between £30 and £40 to carry out necessary repairs. Could it be that the 'new' machine was 'second-hand' when it was presented?

The Government Inspector's Report for 1866 mentions the fact that, in addition to all his other duties, Mr. Deane had recently been appointed as an Inspector of Weights and Measures with an additional salary of £10 per annum. Clearly Mr. Deane seems to be emerging as a very prominent figure within the Borough hierarchy as, in addition to his post of Officer in Charge of the Borough Police Force, he was also the Town Jailer, Officer in Charge of the Town Fire Brigade, Assistant Relieving Officer and now the Inspector of Weights and Measures.

There was some good news for the police in the new year of 1867 when the Government Inspector, Captain Willis, stated in his annual report that he considered the wages paid to the police within the Borough were below the national average, and recommended an immediate increase. Also, on this particular issue it is interesting to note that comment was made at a Watch Committee meeting that recruiting suitable personnel was difficult as a first class constable in the Berkshire County Force got more in salary than the Borough Sergeant. Wages were subsequently increased accordingly. The other issue raised in the letter received from the Government Inspector related to 'Christmas Boxes' received by members of the Borough Force. At a Watch Committee Meeting held on 28 May, 1867, the Mayor stated that Captain Willis, the Inspector of Constabulary, had objected to the receipt of Christmas Boxes by the Police, and had suggested an advance in wages as an alternative. The Mayor produced a scale of wages sent to him by Colonel Blandy, the Chief Constable of the Berkshire County Force and stated that there were in the Borough Force, exclusive of theSuperintendent and the Sergeant, five policemen all in receipt of 17 shillings per week each. He went on to mention that it had been suggested that the Force should be divided into two classes, and that men in the first class should have one shilling a week extra, and, in lieu of the Christmas boxes, each of the men should have one shilling a week in advance and that a bonus of £1 each be paid to the officers in lieu of that portion of their Christmas Boxes up to this time. Superintendent Deane was called into the meeting and, when questioned, stated that he estimated the Christmas Boxes to be valued in total £15/£16 a year, and he further recommended that Pcs. Justice and Buckeridge be placed in the first class category and Pcs. Wyatt, Rosier and Fullbrook in the second class category. The Superintendent went on to state that as Pc. Wyatt had been in the Force longer than any of the officers and would have been promoted to the first class band, but for the fact that he had, on more than one occasion, been reported for misconduct and suspended. The Superintendent's recommendations were agreed upon.

The year 1867 was not a good year for Sergeant Hinds, who managed to get himself very much in the news, but for the wrong reasons. A sub-heading in the Newbury Weekly News dated 19 September, 1867 reads as follows: '*The Police Sergeant on Night Duty -Startling Disclosures*'. The brief facts of the case are as follows: William North, the landlord of the Beehive Beer House in the ' city' area of the town, was summoned by Superintendent Deane for keeping his house open for the sale of liquor at 2 am on the morning of Sunday, 25 August. On the face of it there was nothing particularly unusual about such a summons and the initial evidence involved a third party, who was alleged to have been entertained to the out-of-hours drinking session at these premises.

However, problems arose when Sergeant Hinds, who was called as a witness to prove the case, admitted during cross-examination to taking part in after-hours drinking at these premises on the night in question and remaining there well into the early hours. Most of his admissions came about as a direct result of the Chairman of the Bench, the Mayor, W. H. Cave, questioning the Sergeant personally as he was, of course, fully entitled to do. At the conclusion of the case the Licensee was found guilty and fined £2 and he was also ordered to pay 9 shillings costs. One has a certain amount of sympathy for him, especially as he came in for a fair amount of criticism for allowing the Sergeant to drink and remain on his premises. Without doubt the poor man must have been placed in a most awkward position and put under a certain amount of pressure, feeling obliged to keep on the right side of the Sergeant. The case obviously attracted a lot of public interest, as the newspaper report describes the court as being densely crowded. Reading between the lines, one gets the impression that the sergeant's nocturnal drinking activities did not exactly come as a complete surprise, either to Superintendent Deane or to the Bench. At the close of the case mention was made of the fact that the final word in respect of the sergeant 's actions would be left to the Watch Committee, who were of course the disciplinary Authority for the Borough Force.

The unfortunate sergeant appears to have submitted his resignation immediately after the court hearing. It could well be that he had very little choice in the matter for in view of his admissions, the chances were that the Watch Committee had sufficient evidence to dismiss him and he may well have been given the option of resignation as opposed to dismissal, which has been a fairly common practice within the police service up to comparatively modem times. There is also mention in earlier Watch Committee minutes of complaints being made against the Sergeant, one assumes by members of the public, but the exact nature of these complaints is not recorded.

Sergeant Hinds' name appeared again briefly in the Council minutes a week or so after he had left the Force when he made application for the return of money he had paid into the Superannuation Fund. It was recorded that the Council thought this to be an unusual application, and as such they had no power to entertain it. As a result of Hinds' resignation the Force was left without a Sergeant and advertisements were quickly placed in the local press for a replacement; in the meantime Pc Justice was made Acting Sergeant and a man by the name of Charles Perry was taken on as a temporary 'supernumerary Constable' to keep the Force up to strength pending the appointment of a new Sergeant.

Pc Justice appears to have been a very capable officer as there are a couple of entries in the official records of the Superintendent making special mention of his good conduct and his professional abilities in general.

The new Sergeant, John Handley, was appointed at a meeting of the Watch Committee on 28 September and he took up his position some 14 days later. He is described as being 28 years of age, and, immediately prior to taking up his appointment in Newbury, had been employed for four years as a Warder at the County Jail at Reading. Prior to that he had been employed for two years as Constable with Reading Borough Police.

Throughout this period there was the usual flow of cases going through the local Courts such as petty theft, criminal damage, assault, breach of the peace, ill-treatment of animals, drunkenness, abandoning wife and family, etc. to the Parish and numerous offences arising from the Union Workhouse, but on one occasion Superintendent Deane considered it necessary to bring to the Magistrates' attention the obstruction being caused by shop owners (many of whom were Town Councillors, including the Mayor) exhibiting their wares outside their shops on the pavement. This matter was brought up a second time about a month later and resulted in the Town Clerk issuing a memorandum, one assumes to the offending parties. This appears to have had some effect as nothing more is recorded about this particular problem. One can assume that the Police were put in a rather embarrassing situation over this problem, as the offenders appear, in the main at least, to have been their 'employers'.

In modern day 'western ' films an expression often heard by judges when discharging a prisoner in the old American west is 'Now get out of town'. In fact this, or similar expressions, were used on many occasions at the local Magistrates ' Court when dealing with itinerant offenders, and more often than not a constable was ordered to walk with the offender to the Borough boundary to ensure the offender got well on his way. The other comment from the records, which comes as something of a surprise, is that occasionally the Bench would make an order as to a fine and impose a rider to the effect that if the fine was not paid within a fixed period, the offender would be sentenced to a period in the town stocks. (The last recorded use of the stocks was in 1872, but more about this later.)

Although much has been said by historians about the harshness of Victorian justice, one gets the impression, as far as the local Magistrates' Court was concerned, that it was primarily fair and just in its decisions, and the Justices adopted a down-to-earth common sense approach to their duties: the emphasis in respect of those found guilty was the short, sharp, shock type of treatment, not such a bad thing in lots of respects. On the other hand there were numerous occasions when a case was dismissed either through a lack of evidence or the lack of a prosecutor (Complainant). The overall impression is that it was a well-run Court.

During 1867 there had been problems in Ireland involving the Fenian movement, a revolutionary society committed to the establishment of an independent Ireland, and at the time the government thought that these issues might well spill over on to the British mainland. In view of this possibility, towards the end of December 1867, the Home Office issued instructions to all local authorities informing them that they should be prepared to meet any possible disturbances which might arise during the current winter. It was further suggested that arrangements be made to enrol additional Special Constables so that they could be organised and made available in the event of an emergency. As a result of this instruction approximately one hundred Special Constables were enrolled by the Borough Council in Newbury. As a group these additional 'Specials' came under the control of Superintendent Deane, but they had their own chain of command consisting of a Superintendent and four sergeants (see Appendix 11). The group remained in being for a period of three months, until the beginning of April 1868 when they were officially disbanded. A number of the 'Specials' were also members of the 3rd Berkshire Rifles, a volunteer Militia unit, and Sergeant Cave, the drill instructor of this unit, also acted as drill master for the ' Specials'.

To mark the termination of their services the Mayor of the Borough, W. H. Cave Esquire, laid on a 'farewell supper' for the 'Specials' at the Mansion House after attending their formal disbandment parade in the Corn Exchange. It appears that the supper had been financed by subscriptions made by the Councillors and Magistrates of the Borough. According to contemporary reports it appears to have been a fairly substantial meal and all credit must be given to the Borough authorities for organising such an event. During these proceedings a purse containing £5 was presented to Sergeant Cave, being a subscription raised by the Specials themselves as a 'thank you' to him.

The records indicate that during the three month period of their existence the 'Specials' were called out on two occasions (the method used to call them out was by ringing the church bells). The first occasion appears to have been a simple practice, but the second call-out was of a more serious nature. Although nothing whatsoever to do with the Fenians, nevertheless it involved a potentially serious public order situation, the details of which are as follows: on 1 January 1868 a very serious assault occurred at the village of Inkpen resulting in the main offender, William Teal, the head gamekeeper at Hampstead Park, being charged with wounding and causing grievous bodily harm to the injured party. The offenders, Teal and another man, had been arrested and brought before the Magistrates' Court at Hungerford but were currently on bail awaiting a second court appearance. From its outset the case had caused a great deal of public interest as the circumstances suggest that there was some over-reaction on Teal' s part. The incident did not come about as a result of his official gamekeeping duties, but occurred on the highway near the aggrieved 's home in the village.

The case was being investigated by Superintendent Harfield of the Berkshire County Constabulary and at this stage the Borough authorities were not involved in the issue. However, on 24 March Teal made a visit to Newbury and during the course of the evening was seen in a local tavern. The result, within a very short space of time, was the gathering of a hostile crowd of about 300 – 400 persons outside the premises, each one intent on taking the law into his own hands. Superintendent Deane quickly went to the scene and, in view of the size of the crowd and its obvious hostile intentions, he immediately arranged for the newly formed group of 'Specials' to be called out to assist in controlling the crowd. Mr. Deane first tried to smuggle Teal out of the pub via the back gardens, but this proved unsuccessful. He then arranged for Teal to be escorted out of the town along the Enborne Road, surrounded by some 50 special constables. However, when they got to the borough boundary, the large hostile crowd was still following, so it was decided to take Teal to the borough police station, where he was later charged with being drunk and causing a disturbance. He appeared at court the following morning and was subsequently fined five shillings for being drunk, plus eight shillings costs. The charge of causing a disturbance was dismissed, which was a just decision, as in no way had he been responsible for causing a disturbance. On being released by the Court he was strongly advised by the bench not to return to the town until the main issue had been dealt with. He was then escorted by the police to the borough boundary in Enborne Road. The case attracted much public attention both inside and outside the Court house. Over the following week or so various persons who had taken an active part in the crowd, appeared before the Court charged with various offences arising from the disturbance.

There is very little doubt that if Superintendent Deane had not been able to call upon these additional 'Specials', the situation could have become extremely serious for all concerned, not least the Borough Officers.

A number of changes in personnel took place in very quick succession in September and October 1868, all involving the position of Sergeant. Sergeant Handley resigned from the force during the early part of September having been in office for only 12 months, and the Watch Committee immediately advertised the vacancy in the local press. The successful applicant for the post was John Richard Shaw, who took up his appointment during the latter part of September. He commenced his duties with the Borough Force on a Thursday and was dismissed by the following Tuesday. The records show no reason for this quick dismissal, but only something of a fairly serious nature would have warranted such drastic action. It bears resemblance to the appointment and quick dismissal of Sergeant Rose ten years earlier. Nothing is known regarding Shaw's background, but his appointment to the rank of Sergeant is suggestive of a Police background. Following the normal re-advertising procedure George Goddard was appointed to the post of sergeant on 13 October, 1868.

Sergeant Goddard, a married man aged 27 years was very much a local lad being a native of Brimpton, Berkshire. He had a fairly substantive police background having served in the Metropolitan Police for just over 5 years, followed by a couple of years in the Berkshire force and, as Pc 85, he served at Abingdon, Faringdon and Ash bury. His starting salary at Newbury was £1. 4s. 0d. per week.

The reports of the Inspectors of Constabulary for the year ending 29 September 1868 were published during the early months of 1869 and the report in respect of the Newbury Borough Force gives the following information:

Personnel in the force	8	
Area in Acres	1,722	
Population as per the 1861 census	6,161	
Acres to each Constable	215	
Population to each Constable	770	(as per 1861 census)

The report mentions that two additional constables were taken on for the winter months, but in other respects the force had undergone no changes. The number of reported indictable offences and the apprehensions and committals for trial for such offences were about the same as the previous year, but rather fewer persons were stated to have been proceeded against for offences which were dealt with summarily. The report goes on to state that there were 41 public houses and 21 beer houses in the Borough and the landlords of two of each type of house were reported to have been summoned and punished for offences against the tenor of their licences. The number of vagrants who were passed by the Police to the unions during the year was stated to have amounted to 2,346 persons. The office arrangements were of unsatisfactory character and considerable dilatoriness took place in affording information regarding discipline and state of crime. The duties, however, were generally fairly provided for, and for all ordinary purposes, the Government Inspector considered the Force to be efficient.

During the latter part of 1868 and the early months of I 869 two specific cases within the Newbury area made the national headlines. One involved the so-called 'Newbury Highwayman' and the other case came under the heading, 'The Cunning Woman of Newbury' - a case of 'Witchcraft and its Dupes'.

During 1868 a number of armed highway robbery offences occurred in and around Newbury. When committing these offences the offender was normally armed with a pistol and was masked. He was eventually arrested by a member of the public, who he had attempted to rob in London Road. In the scuffle, the would-be victim, a young man by the name of Alfred Sindle, knocked the offender down to the ground and the pistol went off, but luckily caused no injuries or damage. The offender was then taken to the local County Police Station in Pelican Lane. The offender, a youth of 18 years named William Purdue, appeared at the Berkshire Assizes in March, 1869. During the course of his trial it was stated that he had read various articles about the exploits of the old fashioned highwaymen, and was fascinated by one particular character known as 'Captain Hawk', whom he attempted to imitate. In view of his young age and his previous good character, the accused received a relatively short sentence of six months imprisonment with hard labour. However, before passing sentence, in his summing up the judge was extremely critical of the type of books and periodicals the accused had been reading, stating that the writers had given their criminal characters a ' halo of romance' which was intended to take in silly ignorant persons with such infamous writing.

A public subscription was subsequently organised within the town and immediate area for a testimonial for Alfred Sindle in recognition of his brave actions in detaining the offender. Although the 'Highwayman's' last robbery occurred outside the Borough limits a number of his previous offences occurred within the Borough, thereby involving various Borough officers in the subsequent investigations.

The 'Cunning Woman' case involved a lady by the name of Maria Giles and her partner, William Tranter. Both had been widowed and both occupied the same house in the 'city' area of Newbury. They were jointly charged with obtaining money by false pretences from Isaac Rivers of Hampstead Norreys. It appears that Mr. Rivers had lost his pocket watch valued at £2. 10s. 0d. and had decided to consult Mrs. Giles with a view to tracing the property. Mrs. Giles must have had a fairly strong local reputation regarding her 'mystic powers' for Mr. Rivers to travel all the way in to Newbury from Hampstead Norreys. Various sums of money changed hands and definite promises were made that the property would be located, but the unfortunate Mr. Rivers never did get his watch back. During these negotiations he parted with £2. 6s. 6d. and when one considers the watch was only valued at £2 . 10s. 0d he was hardly getting a bargain. The outcome of the case involved an appearance at the Berkshire Assizes for both defendants. Mrs. Giles pleaded 'Guilty' and was sentenced to 18 months hard labour. Her accomplice, William Tranter, was found guilty on one of the charges and was sentenced to three months hard labour. During the course of the trial it emerged that Mrs. Giles had nine previous convictions for various offences, at least one of which was of a similar nature to the current charges. The judge passed comment to the effect that she had 'made a trade, as it were, of gaining money by the ignorance, folly and superstition of persons coming to you'.

The following week's Newbury Weekly News report implied that not only did the 'London Papers' pick up on this story, they must also have passed some critical comment as to the gullibility of the local population, as the editorial states,

'It was felt that the English public would think that the Royal County is very much behind the times in education and common sense and the town of Newbury

in particular must be a somewhat benighted region to furnish such a mysterious individual as the 'Cunning Woman ' on the one hand, and dupes to believe in her on the other '.

(Reproduced by kind permission of The Newbury Weekly News Group)

On a lighter note, in 1868 a couple of unusual cases came before the local bench, both of which involved the husbands taking action against, in one case his spouse and in the other, his mother-in-law. The first case involved a lady by the name of Elizabeth Wallace, who was brought before the Court by her husband in order to be bound over to keep the peace towards him. The husband, the complainant, was in fact the Recruiting Sergeant for the 76th Regiment of Foot. His wife, the defendant, appeared in court with a 'black eye'. The allegation was that the wife had threatened to do the husband serious bodily harm with a poker. When the case was called the husband indicated that he did not wish to proceed with the prosecution and asked for the charge to be dropped. According to the local press report, the Chairman of the Bench, who was in fact the Mayor, addressed the husband and said, 'I suppose you are too valiant a man to say you are in fear of a woman'. The good Sergeant replied, 'I should think so'. The report indicates that there was much laughter in Court at this point. Superintendent Deane, who was acting as the prosecutor, then addressed the complainant, the good Sergeant of the 76th, and said words to the effect, 'But you came and said that you were in bodily fear of your wife'. The good Sergeant replied, ' Yes, but I wanted to get her locked up for a day to get her out of the way'. At this point there was even more laughter in Court. After hearing from the Superintendent of the defendant's general character, the Court discharged her with a caution, and stated that if she ever appeared before them again she would be dealt with more severely. Perhaps there is some truth in the saying, ' It's a man's world', it certainly appears to have been the case in the 19th century, although this said, it is doubtful the case did anything for the ' macho' image of the 76th.

Another reported case from this time relates to an assault upon a licensee of the Three Tuns Hotel in Newbury, the offender being his mother-in-law, who broke his nose. The Chairman of the Bench passed the comment that this was a sad case and the lady was fined five shillings and bound over. Here again this incident occurred as a domestic dispute between the licensee and his wife, when her mother also got involved and delivered the knock-out blow.

The annual Michaelmas Hiring Fair was obviously a very busy time for the Borough Force and in order to supplement the strength of the regulars, it was invariably necessary for the Borough authorities to swear in additional men as Special Constables. In 1868 an additional eight 'Specials' were sworn in for the duration of the fair and the authorities were obviously well satisfied with the arrangements as official comment was later passed to the effect that the 'Police arrangements were good'.

Shortly after this in November parliamentary elections were held and it was considered necessary to swear in an additional 30 men as Special Constables to cover the elections, which were generally accepted as being troublesome periods from a public order point of view. The decision was obviously a good one as serious disturbances did occur within the Borough during the election period and a number of people subsequently appeared before the Court charged with public disorder and damage offences.

There used to be a common quote to the effect that 'a Policeman's lot is not a happy one', and when one considers that the Borough Officers were still expected to work a seven day week, it is perhaps understandable that such a phrase came into being! However, it does appear that the more liberal-minded members of the public had taken note of this situation and during this period various letters were sent to the local paper suggesting that members of the local Force be granted a rest day, if not weekly at least once a month, and on a Sunday if possible, so that the officer could attend divine services. It appears that arrangements had recently been made for members of the Metropolitan Police Force to have a weekly rest day, but the Borough Officers had to wait a bit longer before they received similar 'time off!

It is always a little difficult to establish the calibre and general capabilities of individual officers of yesteryear when only the bare records are available to assist with any sort of judgement. However, the clear impression in the case of Superintendent Deane is that he was a very experienced officer, having accumulated well over 30 years police experience by this time, having served with the Newbury Force since 1840, and prior to this date he had been both a member of the Reading Borough Force and a Parish Constable. He appears to have 'run' the Force in a 'hands on' manner, being personally involved in the majority of major investigations. In addition he acted as the Chief Prosecuting Officer at least on a weekly basis in the local Borough Magistrates' Court. Considering that he had also been the town Jailer and was currently the Chief Fire Officer, the Assistant Relieving Officer and the Weights and Measures Inspector it would appear that his local knowledge must have been second to none. A good local knowledge was, and still is, one of the most essential weapons m any 'good copper's' armoury.

A case arose in January 1869 which supports the view that the Superintendent was a 'good street copper and thief taker'. The brief facts are as follows: during the early days of the new year, a Mr. Plowman, an inn keeper from Abingdon, called at the Borough Police Station at Newbury to report that he had hired out a horse and trap to a Costermonger by the name of Harry Smith, but the horse and rig had not been returned as agreed in the 'letting' and was now well overdue. The hiring took place in Abingdon, so the fact that the aggrieved came all the way to Newbury to report the incident tends to suggest that Smith was possibly known in the neighbourhood. A few days after receiving this report, Mr. Deane was required to travel to Devizes, Wiltshire, to give evidence in a criminal case being heard at the Assize Court. During the course of the trial he was obliged to stay overnight at the Nags Head Inn in the town and, whilst partaking of a leisurely (and I would suspect, well-earned) drink in the bar before retiring for the night, a man answering the general description of Harry Smith entered the bar and the Superintendent engaged him in general conversation, during which Smith indicated that he had a horse and trap outside in the yard. The Superintendent made a point of going outside to have a look at the property and whilst he was examining it, Smith appeared. When challenged by Mr. Deane he promptly decamped. Mr. Deane was obviously fairly satisfied that this was the property belonging to Mr. Plowman and promptly sent off a telegram to Abingdon to this effect. The property was later identified and collected by the loser. The report indicates that, as there was no warrant in existence, an arrest could not be made. This was no doubt absolutely correct as these extended 'letting' cases were quite complicated to prove at times as although to the layman there was an obvious intention to steal property obtained in this way, due to the 'letting' arrangement, the various points needed to prove larceny were not always necessarily forthcoming, and in such cases the normal procedure was to obtain a warrant before effecting the arrest. This whole incident shows that Superintendent Deane was very much 'on the ball' even when he was well away from his own 'patch '.

In 1869 a number of changes took place in respect of Police personnel. At a Watch Committee meeting on 23 March the Mayor reported misconduct against Pc. Rosier, who had since resigned. At the same meeting it was confirmed that William Stillman be appointed in place of the departed Rosier. Little is known about Pc. Stillman's background other than the fact that, at the time of his appointment, he was already employed as a temporary officer standing in to cover whilst a regular officer was on long term sick leave. He had also served as a Special Constable on a number of occasions. He appears to have been over the age of 40 years, but as Pc. Stillman appeared to be well thought of in every respect, and having previously served as a temporary Officer, the age rule was set aside.

In October the long serving Pc. Wyatt retired from the Force and his place was taken by Charles Allen. Also during this period it was reported that Pc. Buckeridge was absent on long term sick leave and a Pc. Caleb Griffiths was taken on as a temporary Officer in his place. Throughout the whole of the decade there is frequent mention of the Mayor laying on an annual dinner for the members of the Borough Force at one of the main hotels within the town as a token of his and the Corporation's appreciation of their services over the proceeding twelve months, a very civilised gesture indeed, and doubtless much appreciated by the Officers concerned.

Before we leave 1869, Superintendent Deane's report to the Watch Committee during that period gives an impression of the standards which existed in some of the lower class lodging houses within the Borough: he reported that, as a result of a number of complaints received, he considered it his legal duty to bring the matter before the committee regarding the practice of some lodging house keepers who allowed men and their wives to sleep in the same room as young single men. The Superintendent went on to explain that there was no by-law to cover such 'goings on' and he considered it only right to lay the matter before the Council. There is no record as to what action, if any, the Council took in respect of this matter.

In addition to paying a set amount towards the general cost of running provincial Police Forces, it appears that the Home Office also paid for the costs incurred in prosecuting indictable offences. The following table shows the amounts claimed from the Treasury in respect of expenditure incurred by the Borough for instituting criminal proceedings and the conveyance of convicts in respect of same for six years ending 31 December, 1869. The last column shows the balance that was annually disallowed for one reason or another.

Year	Amount Claimed	Amount Actually Allowed	Balance Disallowed
1864	£118. 13. 4	£109. 13. 6	£8. 19. 10
1865	£84. 12. 4	£78. 4. 4	£6. 8. 0
1866	£55. 5. 10	£51. 2. 10	£4. 3. 0
1867	£97. 12. 11	£91. 8. 11	£6. 4. 0
1868	£70. 11. 8	£67. 15. 11	£2. 15. 9
1869	£116. 14 6	£109. 7. 0	£7. 7. 6
Total	**£543. 10. 7**	**£507. 12. 6**	**£35. 18. 1**

Throughout this period concern was expressed by both churchmen and politicians nationally and locally regarding the nation's drinking habits and the Licensing Laws in general. Most towns had some sort of Temperance Society and Newbury was no exception. During the early months of 1870 the drinking habits of Newburians, mainly the working-class section of local society, came under a fair amount of close scrutiny. Locally public attention was first drawn to the licensing issue in Newbury following an alliance meeting of all interested parties on 24 March, when the legislation affecting the sale of beer and spirits was discussed at some length. As an indirect result of this meeting a new association was formed known as 'The Association to Promote the Observance of Existing Laws for the Regulation of Public Houses and Beer Shops in

Newbury'. The association was known locally as the *'Vigilance Committee'.* The main aim of this association was to ensure that the Licensing Laws were properly enforced within the Borough and from the outset it was a far more vocal organisation than the existing Newbury Temperance Society.

The association gained a further boost to its cause when the Grand Jury at the Easter Borough Quarter Sessions submitted a 'Presentment' to the Recorder on the licensing issue and the habits of 'the drinking classes' within the Borough. This report was the cause of much discussion within the local Press, the licensing trade, church and council. Editorials and letters to the editor dealing specifically with this subject appeared in the local Press for a number of weeks. The whole issue locally appears to have been sparked off by the fact that during the months of February and March, a much higher number of individuals than normal had appeared before the local Borough Magistrates ' Court charged with drunkenness offences. One interesting fact raised by the Grand

Jury's report was a comparison between the number of public houses in the City of Liverpool, a very busy sea port with a high immigrant population, and the Borough of Newbury. Although it was accepted that Liverpool had 2,692 public houses and beer shops and Newbury had just 66 such establishments, the ratio per head of population was one for every 166 inhabitants in Liverpool, with its high cosmopolitan population, and one public drinking establishment for every 93 Newbury inhabitants. The Grand Jury's view was that this number was far in excess of the honest requirements of the population. This comparison was subsequently taken up by both the National Press and other local papers across the country. The editorial in the Newbury Weekly News on 5 May, 1870 was concerned as it was felt that these reports may well have created the impression in some quarters that 'the morality of the town is lower than other Boroughs similarly situated and that drunkenness and crime abound to a deplorable extent' (which, of course, it did not).

Not unnaturally the brewers in the town took exception to such a representation of affairs which, they claimed, cast grave imputations upon the conduct of their clients and, with a view to rebutting these charges, they submitted a report of their own to the Watch Committee and called for an open meeting to discuss the whole issue. As a result of so much interest in this issue, the Watch Committee did arrange for a special meeting to take place in order to discuss the licensing issues and the general conduct of the licensed premises within the Borough, but they declined to hold the meeting in public as it would have set a precedent. The Watch Committee meeting took place on the morning of Tuesday, 3 May, 1870 and it was decided that the issues raised were sufficiently serious to make a public declaration of their findings and the following report was duly published in the *Newbury Weekly News:*

'The Committee met this day for the purpose of taking into consideration the application of the brewers for a public meeting of the Watch Committee to be held for the purpose of discussing the statements and allegations contained in the 'Presentment' made by the Grand Jury to the Recorder, at the last Borough Sessions; and having examined the Superintendent and Sergeant of Police and one of the Police Constables, in the presence of the Foreman of the Grand Jury (who was especially invited to be present), are unanimously of the opinion that there was nothing connected with the moral state of the Borough to justify such a 'Presentment', and regret that the same was made. The Committee, however, think it would be unwise to establish a precedent for holding a Watch Committee Meeting in public.

Dated this 3rd day of May, 1870

R. A. Ryott, Mayor, Chairman'

(Reproduced by kind permission of The Newbury Weekly News Group)

Following the publication of this report, the Foreman of the Grand Jury, Mr. Thomas Fidler, issued the Grand Jury's reply to the comments made by the Watch Committee and this letter was subsequently published in the *Newbury Weekly News* on 12 May, 1870:

'The main points raised by Mr. Fidler in his letter were essentially the same as had been originally cited in the ' Presentation', but in addition it was stressed that they, the Grand Jury, were not amenable to the Watch Committee and were fully entitled to express their honest views. They considered it their duty to raise these issues before the Recorder and in fact they would have been failing in their duty if they had not called public attention to the matter. The question of the ratio of public drinking establishments per head of population, as mentioned earlier, was also

covered in the letter, plus the fact that gambling was a common occurrence in various public houses within the Borough. However, the main issue appears to have been the fact that the licensing hours on a Sunday, as they were at the time, allowed for public houses to remain open when divine services were being held. The letter also covered the issue regarding the recent increase in the number of cases coming before the local bench of drunkenness and debauchery. It was also suggested that there were even more offenders who should have been dealt with, but for various reasons they had not come before the magistrates.'

(Reproduced by kind permission of The Newbury Weekly News Group)

On the face of it the whole issue seems to have been a ' storm in a teacup', but licensing was the subject of much national and local debate amongst politicians, resulting in a major change in 1872, when a new licensing act was introduced. This became the main piece of legislation for licensing matters in England and Wales for the next one hundred years or so. It does seem that, prior to the introduction of the new act, the complexity of the old licensing laws made them difficult to enforce in some instances. However, the licensing issue would result in serious repercussions for the new Superintendent a few years later *(see Chapter 8)*.

Sergeant Goddard comes across as a hard working, honest, industrious and 'street wise' officer. He appears always to have led from the front, especially in public order issues, and was a regular attendee at the local Borough Magistrates' Court, giving evidence in the numerous arrests in which he was involved. However, on the debit side, he seems to have been a 'stickler for doing things by the book', somewhat head-strong, unbending and showing little sign of flexibility, which sometimes became evident in his dealings with the general public and with his own men. From about this time and until the force was eventually amalgamated, he appears to have become involved in a number of controversial situations. The first of these related to a case reported in the Newbury Weekly News on 30 June, 1870 involving a Mr.Richard Goddard (possibly related to Sergeant Goddard), the licensee of the New Inn public house near the Cattle Market, Newbury.

Goddard was summoned to the court on information laid by the Board of

Governors, being charged with neglecting to maintain his wife, who had become chargeable to the common fund of the Newbury Union (a fairly common sort of offence during this period). Whilst giving evidence however, Mr. Goddard made rather obscure and potentially salacious comments to the effect that, for the past twelve months or so, his goods had been taken to the Sergeant's house, and no doubt had been used to maintain his family for some time past. He went on to say that he had remonstrated with his wife, presumably over this issue, and he had told the Sergeant that he did not want him at his house. He also stated that he had reason to know that the Sergeant had visited the house when he, the defendant, was absent. What was said at the hearing and subsequently reported, although a little vague, was the sort of information that could set tongues wagging; it was far from clear whether this arrangement involving the Sergeant came about as part of his duties as a law enforcement officer, or whether it involved something of a more personal nature. The published report obviously caused Sergeant Goddard some anguish as he arranged to have a letter published in the Newbury Weekly News the following week which reads as follows:

The Board of Guardians- v- Goddard.

'As I had no opportunity of contradicting the evidence affecting myself given in the case of the Board of Guardians - v - Goddard reported in your paper last week, I beg that you will allow me to ask your readers to suspend their judgement until all have heard the whole of the facts, which the promised proceedings will allow me to give, and which I shall be fully prepared to meet.

Signed George Goddard, Sergeant of the Borough Police, dated 5 July, 1870, Newbury.'

(Reproduced by kind permission of The Newbury Weekly News Group)

As will be noted from the ensuing paragraphs and the final chapter, controversy and Sergeant Goddard often appear to be synonymous.

On 9 June, 1870 a report appeared in the Newbury Weekly News relating to an incident which must have caused the force considerable embarrassment and Sergeant Goddard in particular some unwanted public attention. It appears that a man by the name of Fisher, who the report stated had previously been in trouble, was taken into custody on the previous Saturday evening, 4 June, but on arriving at the police station, he made good his escape. He was arrested again the following evening, but again escaped from custody whilst en route to the station.

Fisher's original arrest for being drunk and disorderly was made by Sergeant Goddard when he and Pc. Buckeridge attended the Eagle Tavern in Bartholomew Street following a report of a disturbance on the premises. Whilst at the station, and prior to being placed in the cells, Fisher made good his escape.

Following his initial arrest and escape, Fisher was arrested the following evening, again by Sergeant Goddard, who located him in 'The Millers' Public House, West Mills. The landlord of these premises was Henry Albert Creese, who it appears had previously served a period of time as a constable in the Metropolitan Police. Depending on whose version one accepts the details of the arrest are somewhat confused. According to the Sergeant, in view of Fisher's attitude and recent past behaviour, he called upon landlord Creese to assist him in effecting the arrest. Creese appears to have challenged the Sergeant's authority and asked to see 'the warrant' and also seems to have questioned the validity of the arrest. The evidence appears to suggest that at the time the Sergeant made the request for assistance the prisoner was not causing any undue trouble. Creese is alleged to have passed the remark to the Sergeant, 'You must do your duty yourself. He then put on his coat and left the pub to go to the Police Station, stating his wish to see the warrant. The Sergeant appears to have made the arrest without further trouble and without any further assistance, but whilst en route to the station the Sergeant was knocked down and Fisher escaped. The Sergeant was then kicked by another man who had appeared on the scene. One wonders whether Creese's attitude and request to see the warrant could have been influenced by his personal police experience - a possible display of his 'knowledge' in front of his clientele? However, as a direct result of this incident, the Sergeant took legal action against Creese for refusing to assist him in the execution of his duty. The charge was heard before G. M. Dowdeswell, Esq., Q.C., the Recorder at the Newbury Borough Quarter Sessions on 9 July, 1870. After hearing all the evidence the Jury retired for just ten minutes before returning to give a ' not guilty' verdict. Local press reports indicate that the verdict was received with some applause from the public benches.

There were some rather unusual features surrounding this prosecution. To begin with there was no Counsel employed to present the case on behalf of the Prosecution. The Recorder explained to the Jury 'That no means are provided for retaining Counsel in such a case'. Comment was certainly made by the Defence Counsel as to the lack of Counsel being provided by the Prosecution, which in practice meant that the Recorder ' had to hold the scales evenly and impartially, but he had also to conduct the case as a Prosecuting Counsel'. The Defence Counsel went on to state that he did not complain as to the manner in which the Judge had performed this duty, but he did complain that such a duty should be placed upon him. He also questioned, 'Had the authorities believed the Prosecution to be just, would they have allowed their Officer to stand unsupported as he now was?' In his summing up the Recorder said he regretted the onerous, disagreeable and painful duty cast upon him, of acting, if he might so term it, in the double capacity of Prosecutor and Judge. It was his sacred duty to protect the law from violence or perversion and to the best of his ability he had performed his duty. After the Jury's verdict the Recorder delivered what can only be described as a bit of a homily to Mr. Creese relating to the law on this particular issue; he also added a rider to the effect 'that in the present case, had there been a conviction, he would have taken a charitable view believing that Creese had laboured under a mistake as to the necessity of a warrant, and would have imposed a light punishment' . The defendant was then discharged. It is a little difficult to establish why no Prosecuting Counsel was employed in this case, unless of course the Borough authorities had been under the impression that the case was not fully ' made out' from a legal point of view and as a result, in order to avoid additional expense, they decided not to employ Counsel.

Unfortunately for Sergeant Goddard, there was still another twist to this saga waiting to unfold. As a direct result of these proceedings, Mr. Creese instituted a private prosecution against the Sergeant for perjury and the case came before the Borough Magistrates ' Court on Tuesday, 16 August, 1870. After hearing all the evidence from numerous witnesses, the bench dismissed the case. The Chairman of the Bench, the Mayor, R. A. Ryott, Esq., in addressing the defendant, Sergeant Goddard, stated, 'That the bench was unanimously of the opinion that as there was no charge of wilful or corrupt perjury established against him, he was therefore discharged'. The report of the case in the following week's Newbury Weekly News states that there were a considerable number of persons in Court during the hearing, the popular feeling evidently being against the Sergeant. This feeling was vented in such a manner as to cause the Mayor to threaten to have the Court cleared. An interesting point arose during the submission given by the Defence Solicitor, Mr. Goulter who, in describing Sergeant Goddard's background and general moral standing, stated that prior to the Sergeant's appointment to the Borough Force, it had been in a neglected state. As one can imagine, this remark did not go down well with the Chairman of the Bench who was quick to refute the allegation stating, 'As I am the Mayor, I think it would be better for you not to go into that point as I have done all in my power to make it efficient and I believe the Superintendent has done so also'.

It is interesting to note that in addition to a full account of this Court case in the following week's Newbury Weekly News, there was also a small article in an adjoining column entitled 'The Case of Sergeant Goddard' . Apparently the 'Borough Fathers' considered that the case had been magnified out of all proportion and that a high profile show of solidarity was needed urgently if they were to attempt to restore public confidence in the Force. The article stated:

'We are informed that it has been resolved on the part of several influential inhabitants of the borough, to present Sergeant Goddard with a testimonial expressive of their confidence in him and appreciation of his services. It has been suggested that the presentation take the form of a time piece with a suitable inscription.'

(Reproduced by kind permission of The Newbury Weekly News Group)

In October it was further reported in the Newbury Weekly News that a handsome timepiece had been presented to Sergeant Goddard as a testimonial to his efficiency as a Sergeant of Police; the watch was accompanied by a congratulatory address signed by 131 inhabitants of Newbury, assuring him of their approval of his conduct during the period of his connection with the Police Force of the Borough. The following week Sergeant Goddard had a letter published in the press thanking all concerned for their gift.

There is no indication in subsequent press reports of what, if anything happened to Fisher. It is, of course, possible that he left the area and was never traced. It is doubtful that the Borough would have wanted to incur the expense of trying to locate him to answer to a fairly minor charge. However, the man who assisted Fisher in making good his second escape and who kicked the Sergeant in the process, Joseph Martin, subsequently appeared before the Borough Quarter Sessions and was sentenced to a month's imprisonment with hard labour.

As it will be noted from previous chapters, throughout its existence the Borough Force was involved in a fair cross section of offences up to and including both murder and manslaughter cases. On the Whit Monday of the year in question William Ward, a resident of Wash Common, was involved in what appears to have been an entirely unprovoked assault outside the Gun public house at Wash Common, when he was punched behind the ear by a person called William Brindley aged 27 years. As a result of this blow the victim fell to the ground and died almost immediately. Brindley subsequently appeared before the Berkshire Summer Assizes in July of 1870, was charged with manslaughter and sentenced to 15 months imprisonment with hard labour.

There was a change of police personnel during this year when Pc. Tegg was taken on the strength, but it is not clear who left at this time.

The year ended on a somewhat 'up-beat' note with an official presentation to Superintendent Deane at the Mansion House consisting of a Testimonial and what is described as being, 'A handsome silver tea pot, beautifully chased, and bearing the following inscription:

'Presented to Supt. Deane by the inhabitants of Newbury, December 22nd 1870 in acknowledgement of the zealous performance of his duty as a Police Officer during the last 30 years.'

The teapot was also accompanied by a purse containing £10. 4s. 3d. The presentation itself was attended by numerous local dignitaries, members of the Bench, Watch Committee and councillors. In presenting the gift to

Superintendent Deane the Chairman sang his praises highly, both in respect of his professional abilities as a Police Officer and as a human being. Without a doubt he was held in high esteem throughout the Borough and comes across as a first rate Officer and a good servant to the people of Newbury. It is interesting to note that one of the many laudable comments made about the Superintendent stated 'That no Superintendent in the County of Berkshire had been more vigilant, or detected more horse stealers, sheep stealers or bona fide rogues than Superintendent Deane'. It is always a little difficult to calculate costs and prices of a by-gone age and compare them with today's equivalent, but if we assume that the amount of cash collected, i.e. £10. 4s. 3d. was approximately four to five times larger than the Superintendent's weekly wage and compare his standing to that of a modern-day inspector, we can then assume that the collection would equate to five times the weekly wage of a modern day inspector, i.e. in the region of £3,000. By any standards this would be a very generous collection and goes to show that the inhabitants of the Borough obviously thought very highly of Mr. Deane.

During the early months of 1871, Pc. Stillman was awarded a testimonial on vellum issued by the Royal Humane Society in acknowledgement of the courage and humanity displayed by him having jumped into the canal to save a woman who had attempted suicide and whose life he saved.

CHAPTER EIGHT

THE FINAL YEARS

MAN SENTENCED TO BE DETAINED IN THE TOWN STOCKS ~DEATH OF
SUPERINTENDENT DEANE ~ APPOINTMENT OF SERGEANT GODDARD AS
THE NEW SUPERINTENDENT ~ PROBLEMS INVOLVING SUPERINTENDENT
GODDARD AND THE WATCH COMMITTEE ~ DISMISSAL OF
SUPERINTENDENT GODDARD ~ EARLY 'FEELERS' IN RESPECT OF
AMALGAMATION WITH BERKSHIRE COUNTY CONSTABULARY

In addition to the normal run-of-the-mill cases appearing at the local Courts, in 1871 the whole Force was provided with some new equipment. The Watch Committee purchased good quality boots at 16 shillings per pair and helmets costing eleven shillings and six pence each. The only other noteworthy event was that the Police were instructed to look into the problems caused by stall holders obstructing the roadway on market days.

Before leaving 1871 a few facts recorded in the Government Inspector's Report for that year are worth mentioning. The recent Census numbered the population of the Borough at 6,602. in the Government Inspector's Reports dating from 1860 - 1866 one of the Borough Constables is listed as a second-class Constable, receiving only 7 shillings per week. The 1867 Report records that the same man was down-graded to a third-class Constable, still receiving 7 shillings per week. However, the Inspector reported in 1871 that this Officer was then a sixth-class Constable and, for the first time, made specific mention of him as follows:

'In the Return of the Police Force, the Corporation include one constable at 7 shillings per week who is the Town Sergeant* and Town Crier and who does not wear the regular Police uniform. The man is always paraded for inspection, but I doubt whether he can fairly be considered as a 'bona fide' policeman and I have so informed the Corporation.'

* This term is an honorary title and should not be confused with the police rank of Sergeant.

In the same report the Inspector also comments on the condition of cell accommodation within the Borough and noted that the 'lock-up places' were boarded buildings formed from the old workhouse and were 'not unsuitable for the temporary detention of prisoners '.

On 17 January, 1872 one of the Night Constables, William Buckeridge, was appointed Town Crier and Bill Poster for which he would be paid seven shillings per week and would perform general Police duties for at least four hours each day. (One assumes that he was paid an additional sum for his time spent on Police duty.) However, either he was not suitable for the job or the job did not suit him, for only two weeks later on 30 January the Committee appointed John Goodchild to take on these duties. These changes were brought about by the sudden death of Pc. Beck on 9th January 1872. Pc. Beck had held the office of Town Crier, Bill Poster and Bellman since the formation of the Force. (*See Appendix xv for obituary*). At the same meeting Pc. Fullbrook of the Night Section was promoted to Constable 1st Class.

These changes appear to be a direct result of the Government Inspector's comments and recommendations which also resulted in the subsequent reduction in the strength of the Force to only seven Officers, a fact which is mentioned in the Inspector's 1872 Report.

It is apparent that throughout this period the Watch Committee had been liaising with Borough Forces in surrounding areas regarding their respective rates of pay. Information received from Basingstoke, Maidenhead, Reading and Marlborough was tabled for discussion at a meeting on 3 July when it was agreed to adopt the criteria employed by Basingstoke as being the fairest and consequently all members of the Newbury Force were awarded an increase of one shilling per week.

Also in 1872 the Town Justices imposed a sentence generally viewed as being more in keeping with the Tudor period than the Victorian age, when they ordered Mark Tuck, who is described as being a Rag and Bone Dealer, to be detained in the town stocks for four hours, after finding him guilty of being drunk and creating a disturbance in the parish church. It seems he had a number of previous convictions and had served periods of time in Reading jail. Contemporary reports state that the Magistrates tempered justice with mercy for, as it was a pouring wet day, the stocks were not set up in the open in the Market Place, but instead were placed under cover in the poultry market with a Constable stationed close by to ensure that the prisoner was neither molested nor treated to any further indignity. The experience appears to have had some effect as the prisoner had to sustain some four hours of unsavoury comment and ridicule. This was quite possibly the last occasion when stocks were used as a judicial punishment in the United Kingdom.

The year 1873 saw a number of changes within the Borough Police establishment. The first to go was Pc Justice, who resigned as a result of ill-health. Pc Justice appears to have been an army veteran and, although it is, not clearly documented, it seems that he sustained wounds prior to joining the Police. The council awarded him a pension of 1 0/6d per week, but he died the following year aged 53, so did not enjoy it for long. William Church, aged 35 years, was appointed as a constable in place of Pc Justice but he tendered his resignation in October 1873 just five months later following an allegation of being intoxicated whilst on duty. Pc Goodchild resigned and Jeremiah Barrett, aged 30 years, was appointed in his place.

Superintendent Deane, who had been suffering from ill-health for some considerable time, died at the age of 67 on 25th August, 1873. He was a highly respected officer who received a testimonial from the people of Newbury in 1870 in recognition of his services (*see Chapter 7*).

George Deane served as Sergeant, Superintendent and Town Jailer; at the time of his death he was also in charge of the town's Fire Brigade as well as being Inspector of Weights and Measures and Assistant Relieving Officer. Throughout his 33 years in the Force he proved to be not only a good and loyal servant of the borough but also a thoroughly practical 'copper'. He was truly a man above the average and must surely quality as having been the main character within the Force.

Sergeant Goddard was appointed to Superintendent in place of Mr. Deane on 10 September, 1873. It is interesting to note that no additional duties were required of this Officer, other than a nominal appointment as Deputy Governor of the Borough Jail. At the same meeting there was some consternation over the fact that a reward of 10 shillings had been paid to Pc Fullbrook for his actions in arresting an army deserter, when in actual fact it was Sergeant Connell of the local Militia unit who had made the arrest. Presumably the Constable was required to hand over the reward money to Sergeant Connell.

As a result of Sergeant Goddard's promotion to the rank of Superintendent, Pc Stillman was promoted Sergeant in his place. The Government Inspector's annual report of 1873 following his inspection found the Force to be efficient and noted that it consisted of a total of seven men covering an area of 216 acres per man and with a population of 943 inhabitants to each Constable. The amount held in the Superannuation Fund amounted to £301. 4s. 6d. Amongst his other comments it was recorded that there were 39 licensed public houses and 22 beer houses within the Borough. (With a population of about 6,500, the drinking classes were well catered for.)

The year 1874, the last full year of the existence of the Borough Force was momentous, if not glorious. At a meeting of the Watch Committee on 24 February the Mayor reported that he had had occasion to suspend Pc Fullbrook on account of his conduct. There is no record of the precise allegation against the officer, but the upshot was that he was reduced to the rank of Second Class Constable for a period of six months.

There was good news for the Borough rate payers in May, when it was announced in the new national budget that the Central Government would, in future, pay more through the central grant in respect of maintaining local Police Forces and the maintenance of the mentally unstable. In the Borough of Newbury the annual expenditure for the Police up to this time was between £400 and £500 and a quarter of this sum was paid by the imperial exchequer. As a result of the intended changes another quarter would be paid by the exchequer, making a saving of about £100 per year for the Borough. Prior to this time it was the local authority's duty to pay all costs relevant to the maintenance of mentally deranged people resident in their respective areas, but as a result of the changes the Government would now pay the sum of 4 shillings per head, per week. The consequent saving for the Borough was estimated to be about £100 per year, making an overall saving on the rates in respect of the Police and mentally unstable of about £200 per year.

The Liquor Licensing issue was at the forefront of both National and Local Government thinking throughout the latter part of the 1860s and early 1870s, culminating in the introduction of the Licensing Act, 1872, which was to become the major piece of legislation in respect of licensing laws for the next hundred years or so. Central Government had involved local authorities and other interested parties in considerable research before the Act was passed. The Government of the day was equally interested in the findings of a survey of the English and Welsh authorities to establish the efficiency of the new legislation once it had been established.

There is no doubt that the whole question of liquor licensing and drinking in general was something of a political 'hot potato' throughout this period, with the church and other pressure groups keen to press for their own agenda. As far as Newbury was concerned it was even suggested that the recent local elections revolved solely around the pros-and-cons of the licensing issue. It would be safe to say that the licensing question was top of the domestic political agenda. In common with all the other local authorities, Newbury submitted its official return on the working of the new Act. The return, submitted through the mayor to the Home Office, established that there had been no problems so far.

However, shortly after the official return was made a letter, originated by Superintendent Goddard and somewhat at odds with the Authority's submission to the Home Office, appeared in *The Times* of 4 June 1874. *(See appendix 12)* It does seem possible that a slight mistake was made in the official return, but the fact that the Superintendent had taken it upon himself to write the letter without first consulting the Mayor was, to say the least, a little injudicious of him, and one can safely assume that his personal rating in the council 's popularity chart probably took a sudden nose dive.

Once again the national press followed up the issue and once again the alleged drinking habits of its inhabitants thrust Newbury into the national limelight. In the ensuing weeks there was much discussion within the Council on this issue and the general consensus of opinion suggests that, although the letter was signed by the Superintendent he was not its sole author; this ' honour' was afforded to Mr. Thomas Fidler, who was, amongst other things, the leader of the local Temperance Movement. It appears possible that the official return submitted by the Mayor did contain a possible error, and that the Superintendent was just trying to rectify the matter, but the way he went about it left much to be desired. The whole issue was to rear its head again at a future date, to the distinct disadvantage of the Superintendent. Pc Andrews, who had only recently been appointed to the Borough Force, was seriously assaulted on 24 July 1874 whilst in the process of escorting a prisoner, whom he had just arrested, to the Police Station. Pcs. Andrews and Summersby had been sent to the Three Tuns Public House in the town centre following a complaint regarding the offender's conduct. On the officers' arrival at the pub they found the offender, a local by the name of James Bradfield, intoxicated and using abusive and threatening language. He was arrested and whilst en-route to the police station viciously kicked Pc Andrews in the groin and tried to bite him. The officer never fully recovered from this assault and was never again fit to perform Police duties. When one considers that Pc Andrews was still only in his early twenties, this injury was obviously a serious handicap to him for the rest of his life. The offender was subsequently sentenced to four months imprisonment with hard labour, which seems light for the injuries he inflicted.

This is the first mention of Pc Summersby. It is not known exactly when he joined the force, but he could well have been appointed as a result of Sergeant Stillman's promotion.

It will have been noted from reading the previous chapter, that there appeared to be a certain amount of animosity between Superintendent Goddard and Richard Goddard, the Licensee of the New Inn, in Market Street. On 1st August 1874 a report appeared in the Newbury Weekly News about a case which had recently been heard at the local Magistrates' Court. The defendant, Richard Goddard, had been summoned for allowing persons to drink after permitted hours and the main prosecution witness was Superintendent Goddard. The case was dismissed when the Court accepted the defendant's claim that the persons concerned were his bona-fide guests and friends. Also, although there was nothing wrong with the practice, and it had occurred before, the Superintendent received more adverse comment over the fact that he had employed the services of a local solicitor to prosecute the case on his behalf. It was normally accepted that the Superintendent presented the prosecution case.

However, in fairness to him, as he was the chief prosecution witness, he no doubt rightly considered it prudent to employ an outside solicitor to handle the case for the prosecution. Here again it was a decision that was to raise adverse comment against him at a future date. Goddard, the Licensee, was an ex Police officer, but it is not known in which Force he served, and in view of the facts mentioned in the previous chapter, one wonders whether the two men could have been related.

In mid August 1874 the Newbury Weekly News reported that Pc Fullbrook had been paid £1 by the War Office for arresting Alfred Jones, an Army Deserter. The question of deserters from the armed forces must have been considered a fairly serious issue at this time, as an official memorandum had been issued by Whitehall earlier in the year addressed to all Mayors of Boroughs and County Police authorities, urging the police to give more attention to this particular problem, and as will be noted, the reward paid in this particular case appears generous as it was more or less equivalent to a constable's weekly wage.

Authority for disciplinary matters varied greatly, the Watch Committees being responsible for all disciplinary matters relating to the Borough Forces, whilst in the County Forces the responsibility was firmly in the hands of the Chief Constables. This situation existed until comparatively modem times, the Watch Committees' powers only ending during the large scale amalgamations of the late 1960s.

The first indication that things were not going very well between the Council and the Superintendent came to light as a result of a 'special meeting' of the Watch Committee held on 3 September 1874. The sole purpose of this Special Meeting was to discuss a number of issues revolving around the Superintendent. The official minutes of the meeting record the issues as charges, but they were not charges in the criminal sense, more like complaints which, to the modem way of thinking appear rather innocuous. Present at the Watch Committee meeting were the Mayor, J. Hickman, Esq., Alderman Flint, Councillors Absalom and Pratt and Superintendent Goddard. The Mayor outlined the reasons for calling the Special Meeting and stated that there were four matters for discussion.

The first charge dated 22 August 1874 related to the Superintendent's alleged comments during the course of a Court hearing when the local magistrates dealt with the case of Richard Goddard, Licensee of the New Inn. It was alleged that during the course of the hearing Mr. Dellor, who was present in the court, lent the Prosecuting Solicitor a copy of the new Licensing Act. For some reason or other, the Superintendent appeared to take umbrage at Mr. Dellor's intervention and indicated that if Dellor did not sit down, he would have him thrown out of court. It was generally agreed by the committee that if the Superintendent had a comment like this to make he should have directed it through the Bench for a decision, should one be required. The Superintendent assured the committee that this sort of comment would not occur again. (It had earlier been decided by the committee that this complaint was not of sufficient importance on its own to call a Special Meeting.) There also appears to have been some long-standing ill-feeling between Mr. Dellor and the Superintendent, both men having 'crossed swords' on previous issues.

The second charge / complaint related to an attempt to extract money from a Mr. Hayward of the Marsh. It was recorded in the minutes that this matter had now been settled. No further action was taken in respect of this issue and there are no recorded details of the facts.

The third charge / complaint was headed, 'Mrs. Gilmore's gift - Not Dispensed'. It appears that Mrs. Gilmore, who one assumes was the wife of a local businessman, had donated a sum of money so that all the members of the Force could enjoy an official dinner entirely at her expense. Perhaps this was some sort of an official 'thank you' for services rendered. The dinner took place at the Jail and Mrs. Goddard, the Superintendent's wife, purchased and

cooked the food. It was agreed that anything left over would be hers for the trouble incurred in cooking the meal. The records state that the men had expressed themselves well satisfied with their entertainment, and they had nothing to complain about. One assumes however, that this complaint could only have come from an officer within the Force, as opposed to any outside party. There was nothing further recorded in the official minutes as to whether or not this allegation was ever substantiated.

The fourth charge / complaint related to an allegation that the Superintendent was alleged to have threatened a local licensee by the name of Collins, that he would 'do away with' his Licence. In respect of this complaint, the Superintendent stated that the reason why he had occasion to speak to Collins was due to the fact that on one occasion he had found a woman crying bitterly outside Collins's premises and, when asked what the matter was, she had said that she wished that the Police would 'Look after that house' (indicating Collins's premises) as her husband frequently drank there and never brought home any money. On another occasion he saw seven men in the garden and one assumes that they were drinking out of hours. Here again nothing further was recorded in the Minutes of the meeting to indicate the outcome of this allegation.

Although at the start of this Special Meeting the Mayor had indicated that there were four matters to be discussed, various other matters were raised during the course of the meeting. A fifth allegation against the Superintendent related to a gift of half a sovereign given to him by the Reverent W. Banting. This gift appears to be in respect of extra duties performed by members of the Force and could have related to officers being on duty at the County Ball. When the gift was handed over it was suggested by the Rev. Banting that it should be distributed amongst the officers concerned at the Superintendent's discretion. The allegation was that the Superintendent had paid two constables the sum of 1/6d each and retained 7 shillings for himself.

In his defence the Superintendent stated that he thought in actual fact he had paid three officers out of this gift. He went on to state that, as far as he was aware, the previous Superintendent had been given a personal gift of 7/6d in respect of his services at this type of event.

Again there is nothing recorded in the Minutes as to whether or not the Committee came to any decision on this allegation, and once again one has to assume that the complaint must have come from an officer as opposed to an outside source.

At the same Special Meeting of the Watch Committee comments were made by the Superintendent who had brought disciplinary charges against Pc Batt for eating and drinking whilst off duty in the Eagle Tavern in Bartholomew Street.

It appears that he had had cause to visit the tavern whilst making enquiries into another unrelated matter and, on locating Pc Batt in the bar, he called him outside and told him that he should not frequent the Eagle, but should go to a 'respectable house' for his refreshments. In his evidence to the Committee the Superintendent stated that he had frequently complained about these particular licensed premises regarding breaches of the Licensing Law with regard to Sunday opening, particularly as it was known that the premises were frequented by convicted thieves and prostitutes. The Superintendent further stated that 'Women were frequently seen sitting with their arms around the men'.

Although not officially amounting to a complaint, the issue over the Superintendent's letter written to *The Times* newspaper was raised again; the Superintendent expressed his regret and explained the circumstances. The Committee was unanimously of the opinion that the Superintendent had acted injudiciously in writing such a letter without first consulting the Mayor and at the dictation of other parties.

From a modem stance the so-called 'charges' brought against the Superintendent were flimsy and one can but surmise that the main issue behind everything was the letter to *The Times* newspaper, an issue that obviously rankled with the majority of the councillors.

At that meeting the Superintendent brought a charge against Pc Buckeridge for being drunk whilst on duty, but this was subsequently withdrawn. There were various other minor bits-and pieces discussed, such as the Councillors' receipt of late notification of meetings, it being the Police's responsibility to deliver the notices to the Councillors' homes, and the Superintendent was obliged to 'defend his corner' over this somewhat trivial allegation. He explained that, to his knowledge, there had only been two occasions involving late delivery of the notices. No decision on these allegations was minuted and the issue was adjourned until the next quarterly meeting of the Watch Committee. Surprisingly none of the issues raised managed to get into the public domain at this stage. However, things were to change dramatically following the scheduled quarterly meeting on 13 October, 1874 when a full report of the proceedings was published in the Newbury Weekly News of 15 October under the heading 'The Superintendent of Police- Stormy Proceedings'.

The meeting appears to have got underway with the reading of a full report of the discussions of the earlier Special Meeting, outlining all the 'charges' made against the Superintendent and the following resolution was issued:

'That the Committee were unanimously of the opinion that Superintendent Goddard had acted very injudiciously in writing such a letter (to The Times) at the dictation of other parties without first consulting the Mayor.'

A motion was submitted at this stage of the proceedings suggesting that the Superintendent should be called upon to resign and a debate followed. It is interesting to note that no discussion or decision appears to have been taken in respect of the other matters raised against the Superintendent at the emergency meeting, but the Mayor, speaking in the Superintendent's favour, stated that Mr. Banting had explained that he had given the half sovereign to the Superintendent to distribute as he thought proper. The Mayor also reported that Mr. Walter Money (who appears to have been the well-known and highly respected local historian) had complained that Mrs. Gilmore's name had been used in an unwarrantable manner, suggesting that the two parties involved in providing 'gifts ' to the Police were somewhat unhappy at being made the subject of disciplinary action against the Superintendent.

These comments appear to reinforce the view that these two allegations had arisen from within the ranks of the Force. During the course of this meeting very strong and personal views were aired both for and against the Superintendent. Some of the anti-comments were that he showed great indiscretion engendering bad feeling in the town against himself, and that there was an intense feeling of dissatisfaction against him in all quarters. It was also suggested that he was under the influence of the 'fanatical notions' of outside parties. This comment obviously referred to the 'anti-drinking brigade' in the form of the local Temperance Society. Another adverse comment aired was that whenever the Committee advertised for Police Constables they could not get the men they wanted because the name of the Superintendent was in ' such bad odour' and no-one was prepared to serve under him. Various members of the Committee spoke up in favour of the Superintendent and his main 'champion' was Mr. Lucas, a local solicitor, who claimed that the town appeared to have been ransacked for anything which might be used against the Superintendent. He went on to state that it was a most cruel persecution to which any public figure was likely to be subjected and that when he had been the Sergeant he had had to put up with opposition from the late Superintendent and insubordination from the Constables, whom he kept up to their duties. It was further stated that the Superintendent had always shown that he was most anxious to do his duty and if, under peculiar circumstances, he had overstepped discretion, he was unlikely to do so again. (This last comment was obviously a reference to the letter to 'The Times'.) Mr. Lucas called for no such severe measures as proposed to be taken. Alderman Jackson, who was also a Borough Magistrate, spoke well on behalf of the Superintendent stating that he had never lost his confidence and he thought that he had been unduly 'put upon'. He went on to state that he had always found the Superintendent to be respectful, courteous and attentive to his duties, and that the Borough was not likely to get another who would do his duty better. Throughout the meeting various members aired their views either for or against the Superintendent. Mr. Lucas proposed an amendment to the resolution against the requirement for the Superintendent's resignation. The Mayor then put this motion to the Committee and a total of four members voted for the amendment, namely that the Superintendent should not be called upon to resign. A total of eight members backed the original motion that he should be called upon to resign. The Mayor and one Alderman abstained and the motion was therefore carried. The question of what would happen if the Superintendent declined to resign was discussed and it was generally agreed that he would have to be dismissed.

During his time with the Borough, the Superintendent appears to have done his job well, enforcing the law rigorously, especially the Liquor Licensing Laws, which may have been one of the 'bones of contention' . Some of the criticism against him was that he antagonised the so-called 'better class drinking establishments' in the town, who obviously felt that they should not be treated in the same manner as the 'lower-class ' establishments.

A number of the town's Public Houses were owned by local brewers who exercised considerable influence on the local economy, thereby wielding substantial power in the community and the Superintendent did himself no favours in 'ruffling their feathers'.

Understandably the Watch Committee's decision was the cause of much discussion within the Borough over the forthcoming weeks. The Newbury Weekly News printed a long letter from Mr. Thomas Fidler explaining his position and giving an account of the general circumstances surrounding 'that letter to The Times' . The same edition contained another long letter from Mr. Charles Lucas, the Councillor and chief Goddard supporter. His letter rebutted the criticism that the Superintendent had employed his services as a solicitor to conduct the prosecution against Goddard (the licensee). He pointed out that this was not a unique and isolated situation, citing previous occasions when other solicitors in the town had been similarly employed when licensing prosecutions were undertaken on behalf of the police. Both these writers were supportive of the Superintendent and considered that the Watch Committee had treated him harshly.

This whole saga was raised again at a subsequent full Council meeting and was reported at some length in the Newbury Weekly News dated 29 October 1874. Councillor Absalom, the prime mover against the Superintendent, is reported as stating that he wished to vindicate his conduct in respect of the Superintendent. He went on to state that he had been accused of gross persecution in bringing forward the original motion calling upon the Superintendent to resign, but he repeated that he did it simply out of a sense of duty because numerous complaints had been received from time to time showing the Force to be in a very unsatisfactory condition. A long discussion ensued , during the course of which Councillor Pratt complained that Councillor Absalom, as a member of the Watch Committee, 'had not communicated his intentions' to the other members of the Committee before bringing his resolution forward, and indeed he seems to have changed his mind between the Committee and the Council Meeting, for on leaving the former, Mr. Absalom was heard to remark, 'There were a lot of trumpery charges', referring to the matters that had been heard against the Superintendent. Councillor Pratt stated that,

'If they were to have a superintendent who was to be amenable to publicans and those who attended public houses, and complaints coming from such quarters were

to be reasons for his dismissal, they would not get respectable men to come forward for such office. If they were to have a superintendent of Police who would satisfy the publicans and those who attended public houses they must have a man open to be bribed by a pint of beer. Because Goddard was not such a man he was hated and they strove to turn him out of his place.'

The matter evoked yet more discussion during the ensuing weeks, both inside the Council Chamber and in the letter columns of the *Newbury Weekly News*. The Mayor, J. F. Hickrnan Esq., obviously thought it necessary to write personally to the paper in reply to Mr. Fidler's previously published letter regarding the now infamous letter to *The Times*. Various accounts give an impression that the original motion calling for the Superintendent's removal was rather 'sprung' upon the Watch Committee without any prior sounding out of members' views, resulting in a decision being made under rather hurried circumstances. Once a decision had been taken there was no going back. Without a shadow of a doubt the real cause of the Superintendent's downfall was due to him sending 'that letter' to *The Times*.

Official Council circles were buzzing with another major issue, the proposed amalgamation of the Borough Force with the Berkshire County Constabulary, but more about this later. Also during this time there was mention in the local press of the appointment of Pc Taylor to the Borough Force.

Notwithstanding the fact that major changes were being proposed, both in respect of the Superintendent and the existence of the Force itself in so far as its independence was concerned, the everyday basic police work still had to go on. The annual arrival of the Michaelmas Fair was always a very busy time for the Police and the Borough Council normally employed a number of additional Special Constables to assist the regulars during this period. A very good description of the fair was given in the *Newbury Weekly News* dated 22 October 1874 as follows:

'The Michaelmas Hiring Fair last Thursday was what is known as a 'Full Fair'. There were shows, stalls, shooting galleries and roundabouts in abundance, so much

so that the area of the Market Place was covered as it is rarely seen, and the streets were thronged during the day by crowds of people from the country. The servants who came to be hired stood in the Market Place. Domestic servants were fairly numerous, and all who could produce good characters and showed an aptitude for work were readily engaged at wages varying from £6 to £12. Carters and Ploughboys were in large request. The wages offered to carters ranged from 6/- to 10/6. A week; under carters 6 - 10/6d; boys 5/- to 7/6d; and in all these cases the usual Michaelmas money must be added, which ranged from 30/- to £5. Shepherds were engaged from 12 to 16/- per week according to the size of the flock.

Towards the evening the country visitors returned home in large numbers and their places at the fair were taken by the inhabitants of the town and neighbourhood. There was a considerable admixture of the rough element and various cases of pocket-picking are reported, the strangers hawking nuts being suspected of plying at the same time such a nefarious occupation. A man who was caught picking a pocket was sent to gaol and among the losses is that of a tradesman who lost a gold watch while walking through the fair to the Post Office, and that of a farmer who was robbed of £10 or £12. '

(Reproduced by kind permission of the Newbury Weekly News Group)

In early November, a rather amusing article appeared in the Newbury Weekly News. It appears that following the recently held Municipal Elections the successful candidates were serenaded by the Newbury Brass Band and the Church Choir Drum and Fife Band. The latter were fortunate in obtaining 5/- from Mr. Adey, one of the successful candidates, who was in fact the Mayor Elect. Their right to the whole of this sum was challenged by the Brass Band, and a melee ensued in which a number of bystanders also joined, and a general 'free fight' took place, but this was happily terminated with the arrival of Superintendent Goddard and Pc Tegg.

Although the Superintendent was more or less under notice of dismissal, he still appears to have carried out his duties in a positive manner, as witnessed by the various Press reports covering his arrests.

CHAPTER NINE

The question of amalgamation continued to dominate conversation within the Council and the Mayor had written letters to various Borough Forces within the Wessex and South West areas where size and constitution were similar to Newbury. Positive responses to those letters indicated that amalgamation would be beneficial for the town.

At the full Council Meeting held on 9 November 1874 the minutes of the previous meeting of the Watch Committee were read. Letters had been received from Colonel Blandy and Captain Willis, the Chief Constable of Berkshire and the Government Inspector for the whole region respectively, and both men were in favour of the proposed merger. It is evident that Colonel Blandy had held several discussions with the Mayor on this issue and, as a result of various points raised at these meetings, further correspondence was subsequently sent to both Colonel Blandy and Captain Willis in order to clarify certain local issues. Having agreed that additional enquiries should be made before a final decision was taken, the meeting reverted to the more immediate issue of what was to be done about Superintendent Goddard who had declined the Watch Committee's invitation to resign. In view of the current discussions regarding amalgamation, the Mayor favoured leaving any decision concerning Superintendent Goddard until a later date. After further discussion it was agreed that the matter would be postponed for two weeks.

At a subsequent meeting of the council on 4 December members were informed that responses to the additional points raised had been received from Colonel Blandy and Captain Willis, and these were read to the meeting. It was then agreed that, in principle at least, that the amalgamation would be a positive way forward and arrangements were made for the Watch Committee to submit a full report, outlining its views and the general points for and against such a merger.

The Superintendent was called in to the meeting and given a further opportunity to submit his resignation. This he declined and as a result he was given notice that his services would be terminated on 2 January 1875.

The Watch Committee's report regarding the proposed amalgamation was read to a full Council meeting held on 9 December 1874 (see Appendix 14 for full details) and, following a very full discussion, a vote was taken which supported the proposed amalgamation. Thereafter most discussions in Council circles were confined to the 'basics' of the merger. A very 'upbeat' editorial appeared in the *Newbury Weekly News* on 5 January 1875 as follows:

'We believe it is the intention of the Chief Constable to station in Newbury some of his best and most reliable men, and that the Superintendent at Speenhamland will be assisted by an inspector of considerable experience in police duty. There is little doubt that Colonel Blandy will strive to do his best for the Borough, as he is doubtless desirous that the new arrangements shall work well and commend itself to the approval of the inhabitants '.

(Reproduced by kind permission of the Newbury Weekly News Group)

Although the Council had voted to proceed with the merger, a minority of its members expressed their reservations on the proposed move when the full Council met on 4 January 1975. This led to further discussions during which the Mayor informed the meeting that there was a 'get out' clause in place which could, in the event that the Borough authority was not entirely satisfied with the new arrangements after a period of six months, allow the Borough to revert to its former status. Superintendent Goddard's notice had been scheduled to take effect on 2 January but the Mayor informed the meeting that he had, nevertheless, asked the Superintendent to continue in office until such time as the amalgamation came into effect.

A question was raised at this meeting concerning the recent conduct of Sergeant Stillman who, it was alleged, had narrowly escaped drowning in the canal whilst being under the influence of drink. The Mayor informed the meeting that he had reason to fear such was the case, at all events he had got into the water at West Mills and, but for a tramp who was fortunately passing at the time, he would probably have been drowned. Although there is no direct reference in the minutes, it appears that Sergeant Stillman was thereafter suspended from duty for an initial period of seven days.

Once again there followed a general discussion on the sacking of Superintendent Goddard and it appears obvious, even at this late stage, that a number of Councillors felt aggrieved at his treatment. The impression given in local Press reports is that the Superintendent, to his credit, was fully involved in local law enforcement issues right to the end. Lesser men might well have just sat back and waited for the forthcoming merger.

It is assumed that the main reason for the ' special ' meeting of the Watch Committee held on 12 January 1875 was to enable a discussion on the situation regarding Sergeant Stillman, who had written a letter to the Council explaining his side of the story in respect of the canal incident. His letter reads as follows:

Gentlemen.

Certain statements made at the last meeting of the Town Council have since been made public, which, if allowed to pass unnoticed, may be the cause of much injury; I shall esteem it a great favour if you will allow me to offer some explanation of them. One of these statement, in answer to a question put by Mr. Dolton, is, 'That on Thursday, December 31st I was drunk, and would have probably been drowned in the canal but for the assistance tendered by a person who was passing '. The facts are as follows:-On the night of Wednesday the 30th December, I went on duty at 9 pm. In consequence of the absence of one of the men I was compelled to be out nearly the whole of the night, and I went off duty at 6 am. At 10 am I again went on duty till 2 pm, thus having had but four hours off duty since the previous evening. About an hour after going off duty, in passing along the towing path towards my home, I slipped and fell down the bank into water so shallow that, although I fell upon my hands and knees, my body was not in the least wetted. This will show the falsity of the rumour, that had I not received assistance I should probably have been drowned. That I had taken a small quantity of spirits I do not deny, but I am certain my mishap

was due much more to the exceedingly icy state of the towing path, and the fatigue
and exhaustion caused by more than 12 hours exposure to the most intense cold we
have had for many years, than to the effect of the liquor I had taken.

Mr. Dolton next affirms that I have been the cause of much of the ill-feeling
lately displayed against Supt. Goddard. I am sorry he should hold such an opinion,
which I am sure could not be supported by the facts.

Mr. Dolton further says, 'He has been informed that three of the borough officers
were about drinking together on 31st December'. If that was so I saw nothing of any
of them and I have no reason to believe such was the case.'

(Reproduced by kind permission of the Newbury Weekly News Group)

A general discussion then followed and there appeared to be some
confusion as to whether or not remarks made by Councillors and reported in
the local press as being made at the previous meeting were in fact made after the
meeting officially closed. Notwithstanding this however, the Mayor informed
the meeting that he had reason to believe that the Sergeant had been drunk and
that he had given some silver to the tramp who rescued him. The committee
eventually decided to continue with the Sergeant's suspension for a further
week after which time he could resume his normal duties.

One has a fair amount of sympathy with the Sergeant over this issue, as there
is little doubt that his hours of duty over this particular period were excessive.
Once he had finished his second tour at 2 pm it seems reasonable to assume that
he was 'off duty' and fully entitled to partake of some liquid refreshment, if he
so desired. (In view of this officer's previous life saving incident one doubts rhat
he was iny real danger of drowning.)

The question of the forthcoming amalgamation, although fully agreed, was
still something of a 'hot potato' in Council circles and there was much discussion
on the disposal of the Borough Police Superannuation Fund. In fact Mr. James
Lucas, a Councillor who had objected throughout to the amalgamation, wrote
a long letter to the Newbury Weekly News, which was published on 4 March
1875, criticising a number of aspects involving the decision to amalgamate
with the County Force. The main thrust of the letter concerned various aspects

relating to the Superannuation Fund, with some very good, well thought-out suggestions. Other issues raised in the letter included the question of the amount of cover the County Superintendent could provide, bearing in mind that he would also have to make provision for when he also had the rest of the surrounding area to supervise. The Council as a whole was critical of Councillor Lucas for going public on these matters prior to full discussion within Council. However, whether individual councillors liked the idea or not was now entirely immaterial, for the decision to merge with the County Force had been made, and that was what was going to happen. On-going correspondence to the Press on this subject continued throughout the month of March, with claim and counter claim as to the proposed benefits, or otherwise, of the forthcoming merger. Even the Town Clerk wrote a very comprehensive letter to the Press, published on 25 March 1875, giving the official reply to a number of issues raised in earlier letters.

Colonel Blandy, the Chief Constable of the County Force, attended a full meeting of the Borough Council on 13 April, when he informed the meeting that he had inspected the Borough Force and that he would continue with the services of Constables William Fullbrook and John Tegg in the County Force. However, the other Newbury personnel would not be required for the following reasons:

Superintendent Goddard - as he had been discharged from the Borough Force he was not eligible for service in the County Force. It was also decided that Sergeant Stillman was too old and would not be accepted into the County Force, nor was he disposed to continue with the services of Pc. Summersby - no reason is recorded for this decision.

Pc. Andrews was not in a condition to continue service (one assumes on medical, grounds resulting from the vicious assault he sustained the previous July).

Colonel Blandy then reported his views in respect of the Superannuation Fund, a matter which had been the subject of much discussion both in Council circles and the columns of the Newbury Weekly News over the recent months. He stated that *'In accordance with the agreement made between the borough and the county on this issue, the balance of the fund, after making such allowances to the present borough constables as shall be agreed upon between the Chief Constable and the Watch Committee, be paid over to the county funds.'*

Colonel Blandy went on to say that his instructions were to deal liberally with the men regarding this. He further stated that the Superintendent, having been discharged, had no claim on the Fund, but if the Watch Committee was disposed to award him a gratuity, he would not object. A gratuity of £10 was then agreed. The Chief Constable then dealt with the case of Sergeant Stillman, who having served for several years in the Borough Force, and on dismissal being ineligible for admission into any other force, (presumably because of his age) he, the Chief Constable, suggested that he should name a sum to be given to him. The Chief Constable therefore suggested a sum which he considered appropriate and it was finally decided to give the Sergeant the sum of £20. Pc Andrews was next to be considered. It appears that on joining the Force in 1873, Pc Andrews was an invalid soldier. Several months had now passed since he had been injured whilst on duty and as yet he had not fully recovered. Colonel Blandy suggested that he be paid the sum of £23 to recompense him for his contributions to the Superannuation Fund. Pc Summersby, who only joined the Borough Force in 1874, was awarded the sum of £4. These arrangements were considered to be very liberal on Colonel Blandy's part and being fully in accordance with the agreement reached between the Borough and the County authorities, they were duly endorsed.

The last hurdle had now been negotiated satisfactorily and the amalgamation took place as agreed on 25 March 1875. The actual hand-over of authority was a very low key affair, with no official ceremony as such. An editorial appeared in the Newbury Weekly News dated 25 March 1875 which reads as follows:

The Borough Police Force

Tonight will witness the disbandment of the Newbury Borough Police. At 9 o 'clock they will walk into the Police Station, lay down their insignia of office, and the county police will thereupon undertake the duties of 'Watch and Ward' over the Borough. The officer who will be placed in charge will be Sergeant Allen of Botley, near Oxford, but formerly of Kintbury. We are not in a position to say who the constables will be, but we believe we are right in saying that two of the members, Fullbrook and Tegg, will be taken over to the county force and probably retained in New bury for a short time, though the terms upon which they join the county force are that they will be subject to removal. The force will of course be under the control of Superintendent Bennett, in whose division for police purposes the borough will in .future be placed.

(Reproduced by kind permission of the Newbury Weekly News Group)

The actual transfer of authority was a rather sad affair and only warranted some 13 lines in the editorial of the Newbury Weekly News dated 1 April under the heading 'The Borough Police'.

'*On Thursday evening on the occasion of the disbandment of the Borough Police Force, a number of men and rough youths collected in the neighbourhood of the Police Station for the purpose, as it appeared, of making a hostile demonstration against the late Superintendent, for when he left to proceed to his home, there was a good deal of groaning and some not very choice expletives. Superintendent Bennett and two or three of his men, who walked behind as far as St. Mary's Hill, called upon the crowd to disperse, which they did, and the streets were soon quiet again.* '

(Reproduced by kind permission of the Newbury Weekly News Group)

Superintendent Goddard perhaps deserves some sympathy, for notwithstanding the problems of the previous twelve months or so, he appears to have carried out his duties in a vigorous and robust manner throughout his service, without undue fear or favour, and to be subjected to ridicule by the local town trouble makers on his last day of duty must have been a bitter pill to swallow.

The Borough Force had been in existence for 39 years and by and large it had given good service to the Borough. When one considers that just prior to the amalgamation the population of the Borough was under seven thousand, and at the time of the formation of the Force it was somewhat lower, the ratio of police officers per head of population was extremely good and the number of men out on patrol, frequently four, during the hours of darkness, has rarely been equalled on a regular basis, especially in more modern times. A modern day Police Commander would consider himself extremely fortunate if he had four men available on a regular nightly basis, just to patrol within the boundaries of a town of 7,000 people.

The mid 19th century was a time of great change, and included a certain amount of public disorder as a direct result of these changes. For example, there had been fairly extensive civil disorder in the Newbury area some five years prior to the inception of the force, when the so-called 'Swing Riots' took place, and the effects of the farm labourers' discontent would still have warranted consideration. Another major factor the Force would have had to contend with in its early days was the construction of the railways, which involved hundreds of navvies descending on the area. The violent scenes resulting from their frequent 'Randys', normally on pay day, are not difficult to imagine! It was obviously 'no picnic' being one of the early Victorian 'coppers'.

Over the years the Force appeared to cope fairly well with everything that came its way. However, like all small Borough Forces it had a number of 'built-in' drawbacks, mainly brought about by the fact that the Force personnel, their employers (the Watch Committee) and the general population of the Borough could, at times, get too close to one another. Once appointed, a Borough Constable remained permanently in the Borough whereas his counterpart in the larger County Forces was moved around frequently, specifically to avoid this kind of situation.

Ever since the formation of the earliest Forces, the Home Office appears to have favoured larger units. Amalgamation of smaller Forces has continued and in recent years there have been suggestions that even larger Regional Units might be considered at some time in the future.

Footnote: As already mentioned, only two of the Borough Constables were taken on by the County Force, their personal details and their future postings are shown below:
William Fullbrook *became Pc 99 of the Berkshire County Constabulary. He is described*

as being 42 years of age, 5' 8" in height and a native of Lambeth, London. A married man with three children. He appears to have served in the Metropolitan Police for a period of three months before joining the Newbury Borough Force, where he served for 14 years. He left on 25 March 1875 when the force was amalgamated with Berkshire County Constabulary, which he joined the following day. His service record with the county force is as follows:

10. 04.1876	*Promoted to 2nd class constable*
12.11.1877	*Promoted to 1st class constable*

He continued to serve his time at Newbwy until 30.07.1880, when he was posted to Wantage. On 20.07. 1881 he was posted to the village of Eastbury. He died on 24 March 1888 whilst still serving.

He had one disciplinary offence recorded against him on 09.06.1879 when he was fined 5 shillings for drinking in a Public House whilst on duty (a very common offence involving Police Officers at this time).

On 22.11.1880 he was awarded a small increase in his wages – good conduct pay. On 25.1.1881 he was granted an extra 1/2d per week in accordance with the new national pay scales.

John Tegg *became Pc. 100 in the Berkshire Constabulary and is described as being a native of Thatcham. Prior to joining Newbury Borough he was employed as a labourer. A married man with two children. He served in the Borough Force for 5 years and five months, and left on its amalgamation with the County Force on 25.03.1875, joining the County Force the following day.*

10. 04.1876 Promoted to 2nd class constable

12.11.1877 Promoted to 1st class constable

He remained at Newbury until 30.07. 1880 when he was transferred to the Reading Division of the Berkshire Constabulary and posted to the village of Sulhamstead. On 13.03.1884 he was transferred to the Wallingford Section and stationed at the village of Cholsey. On 08.04.1892 he was transferred to the Abingdon Division, serving at the village of Long Wittenham. He was transferred again later to the village of Sutton Courtney, still within the Abingdon Division. He retired on a pension of 18 shillings and 3½ pence per week on 19 April 1897. He died on 30 August 1908.

(Reproduced by kind permission of the Berkshire Record Office - Berkshire County Constabulary Records)

Appendix i

'To the council of the Borough of Newbury.'

The report of the Watch Sub-Committee appointed by the Council on the 5th February, 1836, for the purpose of carrying out the provisions of Section 76 of the Municipal Act, into execution.

Your Committee in the discharge of the duty committed to their hands have to represent to the council that they considered it to be one of the first objects of their enquiry to investigate into the system on which the Watching is at present carried out, and of ascertaining the expense of same. For these purposes your committee put themselves into communication with Mr. CHURCH, who being one of the Commissioners under the local Act, for the improvement of the town, your committee thought would be in everyway qualified to give them the information for which they sought. From this source your committee learned, that one Night constable and four Watchmen constituted the whole night establishment of Police for the Borough, and that the duty of these men was to preserve the peace from, in the Summer 10pm until 3am and in Winter from 9pm until 5am and that the pay of the men for performing these duties was for the former period 10/- per week to the Constable, and 7/- a week to each of the Watchmen, and for the latter period, 15/- a week for the Constable, and 12/- a week for each of the Watchmen. The pay to the men and other incidental charges such as oil and candles etc. , constitute an annual charge of about £150 on the finances of the Borough.

Your committee think that such an establishment as this cannot well be carried on, under more economical management, and they have to report from Mr. CHURCH that a rate is in progress of collection that will cover the expenses of the same till the month of June next. Your committee would here observe upon the different walks of the Watchmen which are:-

One	For Northbrook Street, and all Northward of the Bridge.
Two	For Bartholomew Street and West Mills.
One	For the Market Place and Cheap Street.

From these fixtures it does appear that Northbrook Street, when its many ramifications are taken into view, is left without a sufficient guard at night. Your committee therefore submit, whether an alteration of the walks of the Watchmen should be made, or the addition of a fresh Watchman should be made, may not be both desirable and necessary.

It is needless to call the attention of the council, because it is so glaring and so evident to all the inhabitants of the Borough to the fact of the brash shoal of beggars, itinerant tradesmen and match women and boys, with which the Borough is daily infected. This annoyance undoubtedly arises from the insufficiency of the daily Police, or rather no police establishment of the Borough.

Your committee would therefore recommend that a Chief Constable be appointed whose duty shall be to take his post by 7 o 'clock and 8o 'clock in the morning the former period being for the Summer and the latter for the Winter months, and that he shall be liable to be called upon in the execution of his duties until the Night Constable takes his station in the evening. To fill such a situation as this, because of his qualifications for the duties he will have to fulfil, your Committee would recommend, Alfred MILSOME (spelt wrongly with an 'e') *and by way of pay, your committee would further recommend that 15/- a week and a plain blue coat, waistcoat and hat yearly to be provided by the council, should be allowed him.*

Your Committee also recommends that a Beadle be also appointed, who shall have possession of the bell and all the duty attached thereto, and that such a person be allowed four shillings a week and a coat and hat yearly, and further your committee, would recommend the appointment of an Assistant Beadle whose pay shall be eight shillings, with a coat and hat yearly.

The duty of these officers, being in particular to keep the streets clear of Beggars, arrange wagons and carts on Market days, and further, that they place themselves under the direction of the Chief Constable. The clothes of all three of these officers, in case of death or removal, shall be considered as belonging to the council, and your committee submit that John WALLEN, would be eligible for the first and Henry BECK for the second place, and do recommend them accordingly. It may be said that these appointments are expensive, and your committee in reply to this would briefly observe that under the old and present system MILSOME (still spelt wrongly) *had £39 a year,*

WALLEN 5/- and BECK 7/- a week, therefore supposing the recommendation of the committee to be carried into effect the only difference in regard to expenses will be as between £39 and £44 a year and 5/- and 7/- a week and 4/- and 8/- a week. An increase so trifling that it is scarcely worth the mentioning. Your committee have reason to believe that the present night constable is not sufficiently alive to the duties of the situation he occupies, and they recommend that a younger and more able bodied man be appointed to the situation.

In conclusion your committee would further recommend that if possible, measures should be taken to release the present constables and Tythingmen from the duties of their offices for the purposes of appointing other persons in their room.

(Signed)   *Edmund Slocock Chairman*

                John Trumplett

                John Kimber

                M James

                John Flint

                John Satchwell

                Edward William Gray

Newbury, 16th February, 1836. '

(Reproduced by kind permission of the Berkshire Record Office - N/AC.1 /2/1 & N/AC2/1 /1)

Appendix ii

BOROUGH OF NEWBURY.

The following Orders, Rules, and Regulations, have been agreed upon by the Watch Committee, (being the Town Council) for the guidance and government of the night and day Police Establishment, of the Borough of Newbury; and such orders, rules, and regulations, are now published for the general information of the Rate Payers and Inhabitants of the Borough. It is particularly requested, that if any Rate-Payer, should have cause of complaint to allege against any of the undermentioned Officers, that he or she will inform any member of the Town-Council thereof, for the purpose of having such complaint investigated, in order that the Officer so offending, may be immediately admonished to be more circumspect in future, or forthwith discharged.

The duty of the Chief-Constable, is, to arrange the daily walks of the Beadles; to apprehend all loose and Disorderly Persons; to clear the Streets of Beggars, of crippled and maimed Persons exposing their deformities, and of lewd and common Women; to obey all orders of the Council, and the Magistrates of the Borough; to visit the Lodging-houses at least once in every day, and also the Beer-houses, to enforce the orders of Magistrates in respect to their government; and to patrol the Borough continually during the day; and in case of his absence from the Borough, to leave notice at his residence, of the place, where, if wanted, he is to be found.

The Beadles will be subject to the same duties as the Chief-Constable is required to perform, and it is also expected of them, that they shall be on their walks, by 7 o'clock in the Morning, during the Summer months, and by 8 o'clock in the Morning, during the Winter months, and that in both cases, they are to continue on their walks, until 9 o'clock in the Evening.

Every part of the Orders, Rules, and Regulations, above given, and applicable to the duties of the Night-Constable and the Watchmen, are required to be performed by them; and further, they are particularly enjoined to stop all suspicious Persons with sacks, baskets, and bundles, and to examine the contents of the same; to prevent Nightmen from executing the duties of their calling, excepting between the hours of eleven o'clock at Night, and three o'clock in the Morning; and they are also further required, to be on duty, in Summer, from eleven o'clock at Night until four o'clock in the Morning, and in Winter, from ten o'clock at Night, till six o'clock in the Morning.

Chief Constable, - - -	ALFRED MILSOM.
Beadle and Bellman, - -	JOHN WALLEN.
Beadle and Bill-sticker, -	HENRY BECK.
Night Constable, - - - -	WILLIAM LANGTON.
Watchmen,	JOSEPH ALLEN. ISAAC WESTON. DAVID KING. EDWARD WILDER.

By request of the Watch Committee,

JOHN ALEXANDER, *Mayor.*

Newbury, March 15th, 1836.

NEWBURY;—PRINTED BY M. W. VARDY.

(Reproduced by kind permission of the Berkshire Record Office – N/AC.1/2/1 & N/A/C.2/1/1)

Appendix iii

The report of the Watch Sub-Committee appointed by the Council on 5 February, 1836 for the purposes of carrying out the provisions of Section 76 of the Municipal Act. In addition to the previous reports, the Sub-Committee prepared a further report on their proposals for the main duties of the new Police and the management of the Force in general.

To: The Council of the Borough of Newbury

The Sub Watch Committee reports that in order to make for more efficient management of the Police of the Borough and for the purpose of having better means towards the suppression of all disorderly and riotous assemblies of drunken men and women and for the removal of all sorts of annoyances and hindrances to the better government of the Borough that a Committee should be constituted out of the Watch Committee and be called a 'Committee of Managers' of the Police and that each of the said Managers, shall alternatively take the weekly control and superintendence of the 'Day' and 'Night' Police, and further, that in case of any complaint the Manager of the Week shall be empowered to call a meeting of the Managers, or of the Watch Committee to have such complaint investigated and corrected. (The Committee continued with recommendations for the duties of the Chief Constable and wished him to arrange the various duties of the Beadles, etc. These recommendations are basically the same as those described on the subsequent hand bill, which is shown at Appendix 2).

In addition to what they mentioned in the handbill, the Sub Committee's recommendations included that the Chief Constable should:

1. Keep a book and enter therein all the daily 'Walks' of the sub-officers, all complaints from the public, all arrests and charges, etc. this book to be produced daily to the Manager of the day.

2. Visit all lodging houses once a day.

3. To patrol the Borough at least three times a day, one of which must be between

6 pm and 10 pm and be available at all hours, except when he may be called out of the Borough on his duties, in such a case he must give notice to the Manager of the Day of his absence and where he can be found if wanted.

4. The Beadle's duties will be arranged by the Chief Constable, and they will obey all orders of the Chief Constable, the Council, the Magistrates and the Managers of the Day, and they are to understand that if it is required of them to be on their Walks by 7 o 'clock in the morning, during the summer months and by 8 o'clock in the morning during the Winter months, and that in both cases they are to continue thereon until 9 o'clock in the evening, and further they are to be subject to the same duties as those whichthe Chief Constable is expected and required to perform.

A difference of opinion exists as to the person who shall fill the situation of 'Bill Sticker', your Committee therefore recommends that Henry Beck should be the person to execute this branch of the duty of a 'Beadle', but he is to understand that he is not to go out of the Borough in the execution of this business.

The same Orders, Rules and Regulations, under which the Day Police are expected to perform their duties, your committee think only by altering the word 'Day' into 'Night ' will be equally applicable to the duties required of the Night Constable and the Watchmen. These men however, are most particularly enjoined to stop all suspicious persons with sacks, baskets and bundles, and examine the contents of same. To prevent Night men from executing the duties of their calling excepting between the hours of 11 at night and three in the morning. To keep a sharp look out upon the Beer Houses, and to enforce to the utmost extent, the orders of the Magistrates respecting them, because your committee are of the opinion, that many, very many bad and improper transactions are carried on therein. Your committee think that a variation as to the time, when these men leave their duties, is both desirable and necessary because of the depredations which are committed, most of them are done in the morning, they would therefore recommend that the Night Police shall go on duty in the Winter at 10 o'clock in the evening and leave at 6 in the morning and in summer to commence their duties at 11 o'clock in the evening and leave at 4 o'clock in the morning.

Your Committee acting upon the recommendation of the Sub Committee report, dated 16 February, and the feelings expressed at the last meeting of the Watch Committee, have taken upon theirselves in the ordering of the clothes and hats for the Day Police, and in doing this commission your committee hope to have your sanction and approval.

Your Committee acting upon the recommendation of the Sub Committee report, dated 16 February, and the feelings expressed at the last meeting of the Watch Committee, have taken upon theirselves in the ordering of the clothes and hats for the Day Police, and in doing this commission your committee hope to have your sanction and approval.

Annexed hereto, your committee beg to hand in, for the purposes of having the same filed amongst the proceedings of the Watch Committee, an inventory of Watch Boxes, etc. etc., that they direct William Langton, the Night Constable to make agreeably to the 84 Section of the Municipal Corporation Act, and which property, in virtue of this cited clause of the Act, is now invested in the Watch committee of the Borough.

Signed: *Edward William Gray (Chairman)*
                 John Shaw, John Trumplett, George Payne, John Kimber
                 Newbury, 8th March, 1836.

Return of Articles in Charge of the Night Constable on 9th March, 1836:
One Watch House, with two locks and keys
Six Watch Boxes, with six locks and keys
One lock and key to the Mansion House Gate
Two locks and keys to Lock-Up Place
Two Keys to Workhouse and Gaol
One key to Engine House
Ten Watch Coates
Seven Watch Hats
Five oil lamps with straps
Six Staves
Four Rattles

Six Lanthornes

One Shovel to Watch House

One Gallon Oil Jar

One Oil Can

Three Watch Books

Signed: William Langton

Superintendent of Watch

Counter Signed E.W. Gray

Secretary

(Reproduced by kind permission of the Berkshire Record Office

- N/A/C.1/2/1 & N/A/C2/1/1)

Appendix iv

Report to Home Secretary

At a meeting of the Borough Council held on Thursday, 31st March, 1836, the following report was read, and being agreed, was ordered to be transmitted to Lord John Russell, the Home Secretary of State.

To the Right Honorable Lord John Russell, His Majesty 's Principal Secretary of State, for the Home Department.

The Report of the Watch Committee of the Borough of Newbury, in the County of Berkshire.

Agreeably to the 86th Section of the Act, of the 5th & 6th. William 4th. Cap. 76. The Committee has the honour to report to your Lordship that the number of men appointed to act as constables or Policemen by night and by day are eight, consisting of a Chief Constable and two men for the day, and a night constable and four men for the night, and that the arms, accoutrements and other necessaries of the former consists of merely a Constable 's Baton or Staff of Office, and the latter of staves, rattles, lanthorns and lamps. The clothing of the former, which is provided at the expense of the inhabitants of the Borough, consists of Hats and plain blue frock coats, whilst the latter are provided with hats, watch coats and capes. Books are kept by the two chiefs in which they are required to enter all the complaints which come under their notice by day or night.

Further, the Committee have to report that the pay to the Chief Constable is one pound a week, and to the two day Policemen respectively eleven shillings and seven shillings a week, and also the Night Constable is paid 15 shillings and the four Night Policemen 12 shillings each during the winter months and 10 shillings and 7 shillings a week respectively during the summer months.

A room for the Police, and a lock up place for prisoners are provided within a building belonging to the corporation and called the Mansion House or the new Town Hall.

The Committee have the honour also to send herewith a copy of the first rules, orders and regulations, which in the execution of their duty they have made, and it is with much satisfaction the committee have to report that the promulgation of the same gave generally content and have been attended with very salutary effect. In conclusion the committee have to report, that all the appointments above mentioned are in addition to two Constables and six Tythingmen who act for the Borough gratuitously under the appointment of the Court Liet.

Signed on behalf of the Watch Committee.
J. Alexander
Mayor
New bury
31st March, 1836.
(Reproduced by kind permission of the Berkshire Record Office-
N/A/Cl/2/1 & N/A/C2/1)

Appendix v

Plan of Borough Jail

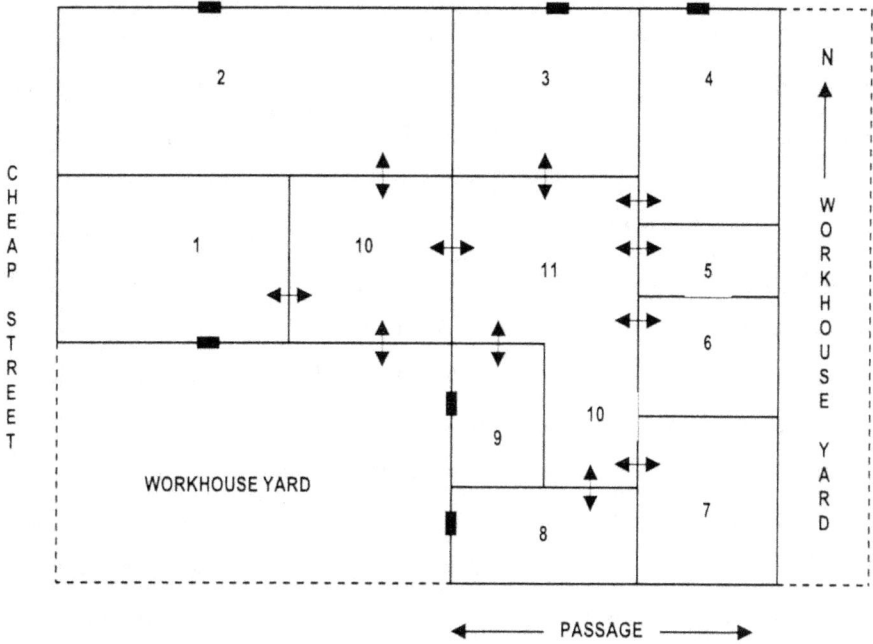

Key:
1 - 4 Cells
5 Listed as a store room
6 - 9 Cells
10 Passages
11 Lobby
↔ Doorways
▬ Windows

(Reproduced by kind permission of the Berkshire Record Office – N/A/C/2/1/1)

Appendix vi

Managers of the Police

At a meeting of the Watch Committee on 18 March, 1837 the Sub Committee submitted its report in respect of the duties of the 'Managers of the Police' together with a set of rules and regulations regarding the management of the Force in its day-to-day operation. The report reads as follows:

It is proposed that Mr. Payne do take the supervision of the day and night police under his control for the coming week commencing on Monday, 6th March, 1837. Mr. Shaw to do the same on the second week, Mr. Grey on the 3 rd and Mr. Kimber on the 4th week and so on in rotation till the 12th May, that being the day on which the Town Council holds its next quarterly meeting.

It is to be understood that the duties required to be performed by the Managers are first to fix the beats of the different officers in conjunction with the Superintendents (The Chief Constable Milsom and the Night Constable Langton) who are to enter such beats within respective books. The managers to receive and sign the reports from the Superintendents, morning and evening of all occurrences which have happened during the hours of duty, occasionally to observe personally that the different officers are in performance of their duty and in case of necessity the Manager of the Week to call a meeting of the managers to take the same into their consideration. And that the duties required to be executed by the Superintendents (Messrs. Milsom and Langton) shall be to obey the orders of the Magistrates, Council and Managers - to keep each a book in which to enter the different beats of their officers and complaints and charges occurring during their respective hours of duty, and they shall under the direction of the Managers, every evening, arrange to enter the beats of the Sub Officers, so that they be frequently changed, and the streets, houses, etc. be patrolled and well guarded- to produce evely morning their book to the Managers reporting therein up to that period all occurrences, including the conduct of the Sub Officers. Any neglect or misstatement herein shall make them responsible for the others misconduct or negligence. Verbal reports of disturbances, charges and apprehensions shall be made by them to the Managers immediately on their occurrence or as soon after as possible, and his directions taken thereon, and they shall each patrol the whole of the Borough **thrice** during their respective hours of duty, one of which shall always be between the hours of 6 and 9 in the evenings.

The business of the day Superintendent (The Chief Constable Milsom) to be confined to the duties of his office, he is to have no other employment nor shall he or the day sub officers leave the Borough without first consulting the Manager on duty.

And the business of the Day Sub Officers shall be, to obey all orders from the Managers and Superintendents, to patrol the streets, homes, etc., from, in the summer 7 and in the winter, 8 o'clock in the morning till 9 o'clock in the evening, both men never to be absent from the streets at the same time and whilst one is at his meals the other shall remain on duty, and from 6 till 9 in the evening and both shall invariably be on duty in the streets. One hour shall be allowed for dinner, and half an hour for one or other meal.

Notwithstanding the Regulations as to the hours of duty all officers shall be liable to the call of the managers, or any inhabitants, at any period of the day or night in case of any sudden emergency and they shall keep to the routes assigned them by the managers, and shall not leave their own beats without the authority of the managers of the day.

The beats during the day shall be Northbrook Street, St. Mary 's Hill for the first and Bartholomew Street with West Mills for the second. On Sundays the Managers to arrange for partially relieving them. Not to be employed out of the Borough, and not to undertake employment of Crying, Bill sticking or distributing, without first consulting the managers. Both not to be engaged for these purposes at one and the same time. They shall account to the Manager as often as he shall require it and to him refer all complaints.

The duties of the Watchmen to be similar to the day Police as far as circumstances permit, to keep to their respective beats, to patrol~thoroughly the whole of the streets particularly the lanes, passages, etc., to report all occurrences to the Superintendent (Night Constable Langton) and to obey both his and the Manager's-orders. The officers shall enforce the provisions of the local Acts of Parliament generally and especially as to *the removal of all obstructions on the pavements and on the highway, particularly in the needless stopping of carts and wagons in the streets, except for the purposes of loading and unloading, and shall report on these points to the Manager on duty, and further they are directed to attend to all orders contained in the printed rules of the Watch*

Committee under the date of the 15th March, 183 6.

Signed E.W. Gray.

(Reproduced by kind permission of the Berkshire Record Office - N/A/C.2/l/l)

Appendix vii

NEWBURY POLICE FORCE.

Chief Constable, Mr. Alfred Milsom; *a.* January, 1835.
Central Office, Town Hall.

Treasurer, Benjamin Weston, Esq.; *a.* 1835.

Inspector and Assistant Constable, Mr. George Deane; *a.* 1840.   Town Hall.

FIRE-ENGINE ESTABLISHMENT.

Inspector, Mr. George Deane.

An Engine is at all times in readiness at the Gas-House Station.

The Newbury Police was established in 1835, and is composed of 5 Constables; its jurisdiction extends over the Borough, with a population of 6500. Uniform Blue, with White Embroidery and Buttons.

CIVIL AUTHORITIES OF NEWBURY.

Mayor, William Dredge, Esq.....*Recorder*, Self Self, Esq.
Clerk of the Peace of the Borough, Joseph Vines, Esq.
Town Clerk, Robert Baker, Esq.

This notice was published in *'The Police and Constabulary List'* in October, 1844 - a publication giving details of all Police Forces operating at that time in England, Scotland and Wales and was the forerunner to the modern day *'Police and Constabulary Almanac'*. Since all communications outside the immediate Force area had to be made by post, this published booklet was an obvious 'must' for any professional Force and one assumes that it was up-dated regularly and possibly reprinted annually.

Appendix viii

Following the report in the Reading Mercury of the case involving the assault of Captain Willes, and on the same page as the Court case, there is a sub-heading which reads as follows:

In allusion to the above case, we have received the following letter from His Worship the Mayor:-

To the Editor of the New bury Herald.

Sir,

Having been made the object of attack, through the malignity of party feeling, for discharging from custody the individual above alluded to, on his own recognizances, and against whom the Superintendent of Police informed me there was no specific charge, I willingly submit my conduct to the verdict of every reader of your journal; and suggest the question, whether the enormity of the offence could possibly call for an investigation of the affair before the Secretary of State - a course to which I have no objection, and from which I have nothing to dread.

Signed William Dredge.

(Reproduced by kind permission of The Reading Local Studies Library.)

Appendix ix

Letter from the Home Secretary to the Chairman of the Newbury Watch Committee

Whitehall.
31st December 1863.

Sir,

I am directed by Secretary Sir George Grey to inform you that he has considered the Inspector's Report upon the state of the Police of your Borough in the year ended 29th September last, and that he has had the satisfaction of certifying to the Lords Commissioners of the Treasury, that your Police has been maintained in a state of efficiency, during the whole year; in the terms of the 16th Sec of the Act 19 & 20 Vict Cap. 69 –

I have the honor to be,

Sir,
Your obedient Servant,

The Chairman of the Watch Committee Newbury

H. Waddington

Appendix x

New Roster of Beats with New bury Borough, as approved by the Superintendent of Police and the Watch Committee

Strength of Force: One Superintendent
One Sergeant
Six Constables (Three day duty Officers
and three night duty Officers)

It was proposed to abolish the position of one day duty Constable and place him on night duty; this Constable would reside at 'Wash Common' at all times. It was proposed that the duty should be performed in the following manner:

No. 1 Constable To commence duty at 6 am and to patrol the whole of the town until 12 noon, then from 4 pm to 8 pm.

No. 2 Constable Who resides on Wash Common, to commence duty at 12 noon, to come into Newbury and to do duty until 4 pm at which time No. 1 Constable shall commence again and remain on duty until 8 pm. This will end the day duty.

No. 3 Constable To commence duty at 8 pm and to remain on duty until 5 am.

No. 4 Constable To commence duty at 9 pm and to remain on duty until 6 am.

No. 5 Constable Duties as Constable No. 4.

No. 2 Constable Will resume duty again at 9 pm and remain on duty until 3 am.

It was also decided at this time to make four night duty beats instead of the three that are used at present.

No. 1 Beat   To commence at the Water Bridge, to patrol down the East side of Northbrook Street, including the Jack Yard, the Marsh and Parrs Yard, to the letter box, cross over Northbrook Street and patrol up the West side of the street, including West Street and Northcroft Lane, alternatively the Marsh and the Jack Yard in the same manner.

No. 2 Beat   Commencing patrol at the Mansion House, up the West side of the Market Place, St. Mary's Hill to Smiths Coffee Shop, then cross over down the East side of the same roads, also covering Back Lane, the Bear Yard, into the Wharf up to the Bridge, cross over up West Mills to Mr. Adeys, down to Mr. Shaws, back through the South side of the Church, through Little Lane back into the Market Place, repeating the process as before.

No. 3 Beat   Commencing at the Church up the West side of Bartholomew Street to New Street, down New Street to Mr. Shaws, back up to the 'Blackboys', along Pound Street to the Lamb, back and through the City to Southampton Terrace, Prospect Place and Railway Terrace, back down the East side of Bartholomew Street to the Water Bridge.

No. 4 Beat   To commence at Wash Common, down the Wash Road to the Police Station, back up the Newtown Road, to the Union House, through Monkey Lane into Wash Common, back down the Andover Road, then cross over the fields down to the Enborne Road, down to Mr. Winsons, by the Rectory, up Bartholomews to the London Apprentice, then go over the beat as before.

All these changes were fully adopted by the Watch Committee.

(Reproduced by kind permission of the Berkshire Record Office - N/A/C. l/2/2)

Appendix xi

List of Special Constables recruited for the Fenian 'Scare'
1868

T. W. Graham	A. Burns	J. J. Roake
Henry James Smith	S. (H) Freeman	E. J. Bance
G. Poole	E. T. Brooks	G. Mayo
H. Bailey	W. Sumpster	J. Withers
H. B. Scard	F. Comyne	J. Packer
H. Meakins	W. Balding	John Burgess
C. Lucas	J. Slade (Jun)	C. W. Marr
R. Panting	W. Dore	George Liddiard
C. Saunders	W. Burgess	John Cooper
G. Callis	S. Flint (Sgt.)	J. Absalom
E. Plummer	H. Attewell	George Crosswell
James Liddiard	T. G. King (Supt.)	J. B. Stone
H. J. Matthews	John Basing	R. Basing
S. H. Looker	W. Wheeler	R. Martin
B. Sargent (Sgt.)	C. D. Finch	W. Knight
E. Windsor	E. Higgs	James Copas
John Fox	W. W. King (Sgt.)	G. Deane (Jun)
J. Langton	E. Salway	Charles Paris
J. Philpot	W. O' Brien	H. Gayzer
George Boyer	S. Elliott	F. Stone
W. H. Webster	W. Hickman	W. H. Jackson
Thomas Newton (Sgt.)	M. Gray	W. Griffin
E. Robinson	E. Harrison	E. Lack
H. Cullen	H. Purdue	T. Willis
T. Tranter	W. Griffiths	S.Biddis
J. C. Pinniger	E. Willis	W. J.Pennington
R. Cubbage	J. Britten	W. Swann
C. Sangwell	S. Thatcher	R. Smith
G. Jarrett	R. Willis	T. Deller
E. Polhill	A. Elliott	S. J. Wilkinson
W. Cook		

(Reproduced by kind permission of the Newbury Weekly News Group)

Appendix xii

The Licensing Bill

Superintendent's letter to the Editor of The Times newspaper published on 4 June, 1874

'Sir,

My attention has been called to the following clause of your leading article of Tuesday on the results of the licensing Act in Boroughs. At Newbury it is stated that the shortening of the hours has probably had an injurious effect, for it is known that instances have occurred in which working men have joined in purchasing a quantity of liquor at the last moment and then adjourned to some private house and become intoxicated.

I am at a loss to understand how such a statement could have found its way into the report from this Borough as the shortening of the hours of sale has, by universal testimony, been most beneficial. Such a circumstance as that mentioned was as common before the passing of the Act of 1872 as it has been since, and if the public houses were allowed to be opened until midnight such cases would still happen.

The curtailment of the hours of public drinking, as stated in my report, has been the means of promoting the quiet and good order of the town to a very remarkable extent; and it is my conviction that if the hours of opening were curtailed, so that men could enter on their day's work free from the temptation to indulge in intoxicating liquor, it would have the most beneficial effect.

I am, sir, your obedient servant.
George Goddard
Superintendent of Newbury Borough Police Force Newbury.'

(Reproduced by kind permission of The National Newspaper Library, London)

Appendix xiii

List of annually appointed 'Specials' and early Fire Brigade personnel

The Force was supplemented by 'Special' Constables who could be used to assist the regulars whenever it was anticipated that there would be large public gatherings or possible public disorder such as fairs, general elections, etc. (During the Fenian Scare a very large number of Specials were sworn in, with their own command structure, which is shown at appendix 11.)

By and large the 'Specials' were sworn in on an annual basis, but occasionally additional numbers were sworn in for special events, mainly parliamentary elections.

Records on this subject are limited, but the following is a list of 'specials' recorded during the middle years of the Force's history.

Exact date unknown but thought to be in the 1840s	**Annual Specials:** Messrs. Henry TAYLOR, Thomas GAMMON
	Tythingmen: John SLADE, John STAPLES, Thomas LONG, William WITHERINGTON, Joseph HOBBS, W. JOPLEN
1849	**Annual Specials:** Messrs. R. BROWN, H. BRADLEY, Jas. FREWIN, William MORRIS, Henry Thomas NEWBERY
1852	**Annual Specials:** Messrs. James FREWIN (also the gaoler), Henry Thomas NEWBERY, William KNIGHT, William BAILEY, Cornelius CHALLIS & F. THOMAS. Mrs. FREWIN- Matron to the gaoler
1853	**Annual Specials:** Messrs. James FREWIN, Henry Thomas NEWBERY, William KN1GHT, William BAILEY, Cornelius CHALLIS & F. THOMAS

1856	Annual Specials: Messrs. James FREWIN, William SAMUELS, Henry HOCKLEY, T. WAITS, James PEN RICE & William NORTH

| 1858 | Annual Specials: William TAYLOR, William SAMUELS, Henry HOCKLEY, William GIBBS & Benjamin DORE |

| 1861 | Annual Specials: Messrs. George THORN, William TAYLOR, Thomas DAVIS, William FULLBROOK, Thomas PURDUE, John PURTON, Frederick STILLMAN & George PAULING |

| 1863 | Annual Specials: Messrs. William KNIGHT, George BROWN, George PAULING (sometimes spelt PAULDING), Thomas NORTH, Thomas DAVJES, W. TAYLOR, J. PURTON & T. PAYNE |

| 1867 | Annual Specials: Messrs. Alfred PEARCE, William TA YLOR, Charles GIBBS, William WHEELER, Charles PEARCE, Alfred HALL & Charles Richard PERRY |

| 1867 | Additional Special Constables sworn in to cover Michaelmas Fair: Messrs. William STILLMAN, Caleb GOSLING, Caleb GRIFFITHS, William TA YLOR, William PITMAN, James CARTER, Charles GIBBS & Alfred HALL |

FIRE BRIGADE PERSONNEL

In addition to his police duties Superintendent Deane was also in charge of the town 's Fire Brigade. Little information available but the following were members of the Brigade under Mr. Deane.

| 1866 | Messrs. TA YLOR (Engineer), G. HAYES (Sergeant), F. STONE (Corporal) |

(Reproduced by kind permission of the West Berkshire Museum, Newbury)

Appendix xiv

Report of Watch Committee presented to the full Newbury Borough Council on 9 December 1874 relating to the proposed amalgamation of the New bury Borough Police Force with the Berkshire County Force

To the Mayor and Town Council of the Borough of Newbury

We the Watch Committee for the Borough of Newbury, having had brought before our notice the very unsatisfactory state of our Borough Police and having carefully considered the benefits and disadvantages (if any) to result to the Borough on the score of economy, efficiency, and general benefit if an amalgamation of the Borough and County Police were effected have as the result of our enquiries come to the conclusion that the Borough would be benefited by such an amalgamation for amongst others the following reasons.

That the cost would not exceed, probably be a little less than the cost under the present arrangement.

That we should never have less than the present number of Police on duty within the borough, and in addition thereto, all members of the County Police on passing and repassing within the borough would be on duty. Also at all fairs, elections and other meetings and large gatherings of persons within the Borough, as many of the County Police as might be required would be sent into the Borough on duty, thereby affording a very considerable saving in the pay and appointment of Special Constables.

That the Borough Prisoners would be held in custody at the County Police Station at Speenhamland at no other charge than their maintenance thereby saving the cost of the present gaol, gaoler, and Superintendent 's residence, also the pay of a Borough Superintendent, as the duties of the Superintendent would be carried on by the Superintendent of the County Police at Speenhamland.

That the status of the Borough Justices would in no wise be affected by the proposed change. And as the consolidation would be carried out by an agreement in writing, provision would therein be made for a dissolution of the contract if its continuation should be inconvenient or unsatisfactory.

For the above, amongst other reasons, we the Watch Committee, on whom the sole appointment and arrangement of the Police are vested, under the 5th and 6th William IV, c. 76, sec. 77, have come to the conclusion that it would be advisable that the Borough Police should for the future be in connection with the County, and we therefore suggest to the Council that they do forthwith take the necessary steps under the 3rd and 4th Vic. Cap, 88. Sec. 14 and 15, to carry out our views and recommendations.

W. G. Adey, Mayor
W H Cave, Chairman
J. B. Pratt
Jas. Absalom.'

(Reproduced by kind permission of the Berkshire Record Office- N/A/ C. I/2/3)

Appendix xv

Obituary to Pc Beck

Pc. Henry Froom Beck died on 9th January 1872 aged 70. Described on his death certificate as a 'Policeman and Town Crier', his obituary appeared in the Newbury Weekly News on 11th January 1872 and reads as follows:

It is not every official whose death is more genuinely regretted than that of Henry Beck, the town crier of Newbury. He retained the character throughout a long career of being a straightforward, honest man, and a faithful servant to the public; in his family relations he leaves behind him the testimony of being an affectionate husband and a loving father.

He was a native of Reading and came to Newbury nearly half a century ago, working as a journeyman baker to Mr. Witherington. For 40 years Beck had been a constable of the borough and for 33 years bill poster and town crier. It is in his latter capacity that he will be best remembered, his stentorian voice being as clear and distinct as the tone of the bell which he rung. So much did he excel in this particular that he has often been described as 'the best town crier in England'. He was gifted with an excellent memory for retaining past events, and was always punctual at his post, even if the appointment had been made weeks previously, and the person making it had forgotten the same. It was evident to those who knew him that for the past twelve months his constitution was breaking up, and the unexpected death of a son about two months since caused him much grief. The last lot of bills that he distributed was for the Christy Minstrels, and he died on Tuesday last, the day of the entertainment, at the age of 70. An announcement for the coal club was, we believe, his last public act as town crier. He will be buried on Saturday at the cemetery, and the Police force will follow his remains.

TOWN CRYING IN NEWBURY

The Borough of Newbury appears to have had the services of a Bellman and Town Crier since 1649, when a local order was made which permitted the employment of such an official. His duties included preserving the town from the dangers of fire and other great inconveniences that were likely to happen and for the apprehension of all pilfering rogues and suspicious persons. In addition to these duties, as Bellman he was required to patrol the streets and shout in a distinct and audible fashion to give notice of various issues, plus the condition of the weather and during the hours of darkness he was to shout out the time. His hours of duty were onerous, as he was required to perform these duties from 9 am to 5 pm and then from 9 pm to 5 am.

It is clear that this official's duties were well established long before the formation of the borough police force.

Appendix xvi

OFFICERS SERVING IN THE BOROUGH FORCE

NAME	DATE APPOINTED	DATE LEFT & REASON FOR LEAVING
Alfred MILSOM (Chief Constable)	15.3.1836	Died 22.5.1852
John WALLEN (Day constable, Beadle & Bellman)	15.3.1836	Retired July 1837
Henry BECK (Day constable, Beadle & Bill Sticker)	15.3.1836	Died 9.1.1872
William LANGTON (Night constable)	15.3.1836	Dismissed for theft 22.5.1840
John or Joseph ALLEN (Watchman)	15.3.1836	Dismissed November 1845
Isaac WESTON (Watchman)	15.3.1836	Retired some time after 1848
David KING (Watchman)	15.3.1836	Died on 12.8.1836
Edward WILDER (Watchman)	15.3.1836	Resigned April 1847
John TOMPKINS (Watchman)	12.8.1836	Resigned April 1847
Samuel ELKINS	First mentioned in 1836, then a final mention in a Press report dated 1840.	No further details recorded
William STROUD (Day constable, Beadle & Bellman)	July 1837	Resigned 21.3.1838
William GATEHOUSE (Day Constable, Beadle& Bellman)	3.4.1838	Resigned July 1838
WARWICK	Mentioned in Council records of 1838	No further details recorded
George DEANE (Night Sgt – later Superintendent)	12.6.1840	Died 25.8.1873
TEWSON	Mentioned in a Press report of 1840	No further details recorded
J. KING (Night patrolman ~ watchman)	November 1845	Not known

OFFICERS SERVING IN THE BOROUGH FORCE continued...

James WYATT (Night patrolman ~ watchman)	14.4.1847	October 1869
Henry WAIT (Night patrolman – watchman)	14.4.1847	Not known
George NOYES (Night Patrolman ~Watchman)	Not known	1847 ~ first mention that he was disabled and due to retire. Appears to have carried on working in various posts to 4.9.1852
John WHITING (Night Patrolman ~ Watchman)	7.7.1847	Thought to have retired 1850
William LANGTON (Temporary ~ Watchman)	15.11.1850	1.3.1851 (contract expired)
William NORTH (Temporary ~ Watchman)	15.11.1850	1.3.1851
John HILL (Sergeant ~ Night patrol)	10.7.1852	Retired 14.8.1857
William BUCKERIDGE (Night Patrolman ~ Watchman)	9.11.1852	Resigned 30.1.1872
John William ROSE (Night Sergeant)	26.9.1857 (approx.)	Dismissed for misconduct 30.9.1857
Thomas HINDS (Night Sergeant)	21.10.1857	Resigned 19.9.1867
George PAULIN (Temporary ~ Night patrol officer)	7.10.1862	Employed for just a couple of months
Charles DEANE (Temporary ~ Night Patrol Officer)	7.10.1862	Employed for just a couple of months
Benny LEWIS (Temporary ~ Night Patrol Officer) Replacement for Pc Rosier	May 1864	Dismissed 12.7.1864
James SAVORY (Temporary ~ Night Patrol Officer)	23.12.1848	Temporary appointment for only 3 nights
James LIDDIARD (Temporary ~ Night Patrol Officer)	23.12.1848	Temporary appointment for 3 nights

OFFICERS SERVING IN THE BOROUGH FORCE continued...

Stephen JUSTICE (Night Patrol Officer)	First mentioned in October 1849 as a temporary appointment, later taken on as a full-time officer (exact date not known)	Resigned due to ill health 30.5.1873 Died 21.5.1874
BRADFIELD (Temporary ~ Night Patrol Officer)	17.11.1849	Temporary appointment for a few days only
Thomas WARNER (Night Patrol Officer)	17.11.1849 & 28.2.1852	Temporary appointments for a few days only
Thomas KIMBER (Temporary ~ Night Patrol Officer) Later employed permanently	16.3.1850	Died March 1861
Thomas BRAZIER (Night Patrol Officer)	4.9.1852 Returned as a temporary for a few days in 1854	9.10.1852 Possibly a temporary appointment
Hugh GAUNTLETT (Night Patrol Officer)	28.2.1852 & 9.10.1852 Possibly 2 temporary appointments	Not known
Vincent WYVELL (or WYATT) (Night Patrol Officer)	21.2.1857	Not known
Thomas ROSIER (Night Patrol Officer)	21.2.1857	Resigned 23.3.1869 (alleged misconduct not stipulated)
SAMUELS	September 1857	Not known Temporary appointment only
James BOSHIER (Temporary ~ Night Patrol Officer)	3.4.1858	Mid April 1858
William FULLBROOK (Temporary ~ Night Patrol Officer ~ later employed permanently)	13.4.1859	25.3.1875 then taken on by Berkshire County Constabulary
DIBLEY	27.2.1864	Late March 1864 Temporary appointment only
Thomas LANGTON	28.2.1852	Not known Temporary appointment only

OFFICERS SERVING IN THE BOROUGH FORCE continued...

Charles PERRY	28.9.1867	Not known Temporary appointment 2 weeks only
John HANDLEY Sergeant	13.10.1867	Resigned September 1868
John Richard SHAW Sergeant	September 1868	September 1868 Discharged within one week
George GODDARD Sergeant ~ later promoted to Superintendent	13.10.1868	25.3.1875 Dismissed on amalgamation with Berkshire County Force
Charles ALLEN	4.10.1869	Not known
William STILLMAN Special Constable, Temporary Constable ~later taken on permanently ~ promoted Sergeant in later years	23.3.1869	25.3.1875 Dismissed on amalgamation with Berkshire County Force
John TEGG	1870 First mention	Taken on as a Pc with Berkshire County Police on amalgamation
John GOODCHILD	30.1.1872	Resigned 30.5.1873
William CHURCH	4.6.1873	Resigned 19.10.1873
Jeremiah BARRETT	30.5.1873	Not known
Henry ANDREWS	19.9.1873	Badly injured on duty 1875 ~ dismissed on 25.3.1875 on amalgamation with Berkshire County Force due to being unfit
Caleb GRIFFITHS Employed as a temporary officer in place of Pc Buckeridge ~ who was ill	23.3.1869	Not known but as a temporary Officer – limited time only
BATT	First mentioned in 1874	Not known – possibly a temporary appointment
TAYLOR	First mentioned in 1874	Details not known but had left prior to amalgamation
SUMMERSBY	First mentioned in 1874	Discharged in 1875 on amalgamation with Berkshire County Constabulary – no reason given

Constable Henry Beck

-a-

Market Place Newbury, Berks

Canal Scene - West Mills

Early photograph – Borough Fire Brigade

Newbury Theatre – Pelican Lane

Early Drawing of London Road
at its junction with Broadway

-f-

Street Scene – early photograph
of Northbrook Street

BOARD OF HEALTH.

PUBLIC NOTICE.

Whereas, complaints have been made to this Board of the existence of

NUISANCES

In certain parts of the Borough, offensive to the Inhabitants and injurious to the Public Health, the Inhabitants of the Borough generally are hereby requested to see that all Nuisances are Removed and prevented, that Water be plentifully supplied to all Drains. Closets, &c., belonging to the respective properties in their occupation, and that great attention to Cleanliness be observed.

Informations of any neglect to comply with this Notice, may be left at the Office of the Local Board of Health, or with the Surveyor.

THOMAS FIDLER,

Chairman of the Local board of Health.

Newbury, 1st August, 1865.

Notice Issued by the Board of Health

1865

-h-

The Market Place – Demonstration of a new fire escape ladder circa 1871

Button from early police tunic

*Tipstaff which may have
been issued to
Superintendent Deane*

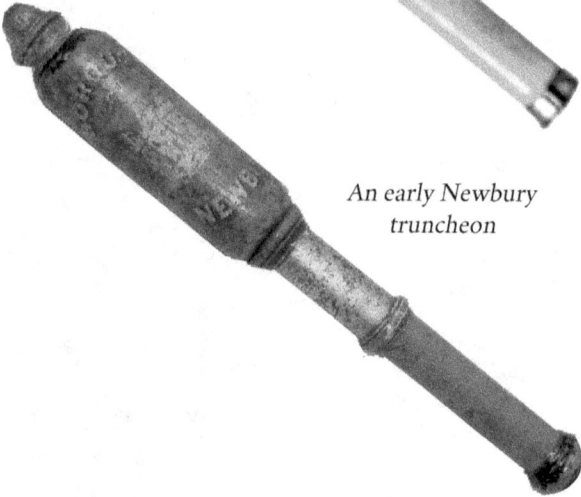

*An early Newbury
truncheon*

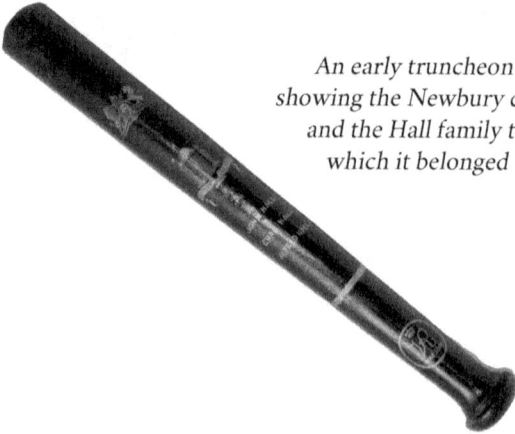

*An early truncheon
showing the Newbury crest
and the Hall family to
which it belonged*

Photo of Mansion House as it looked in the latter days of the Borough Force

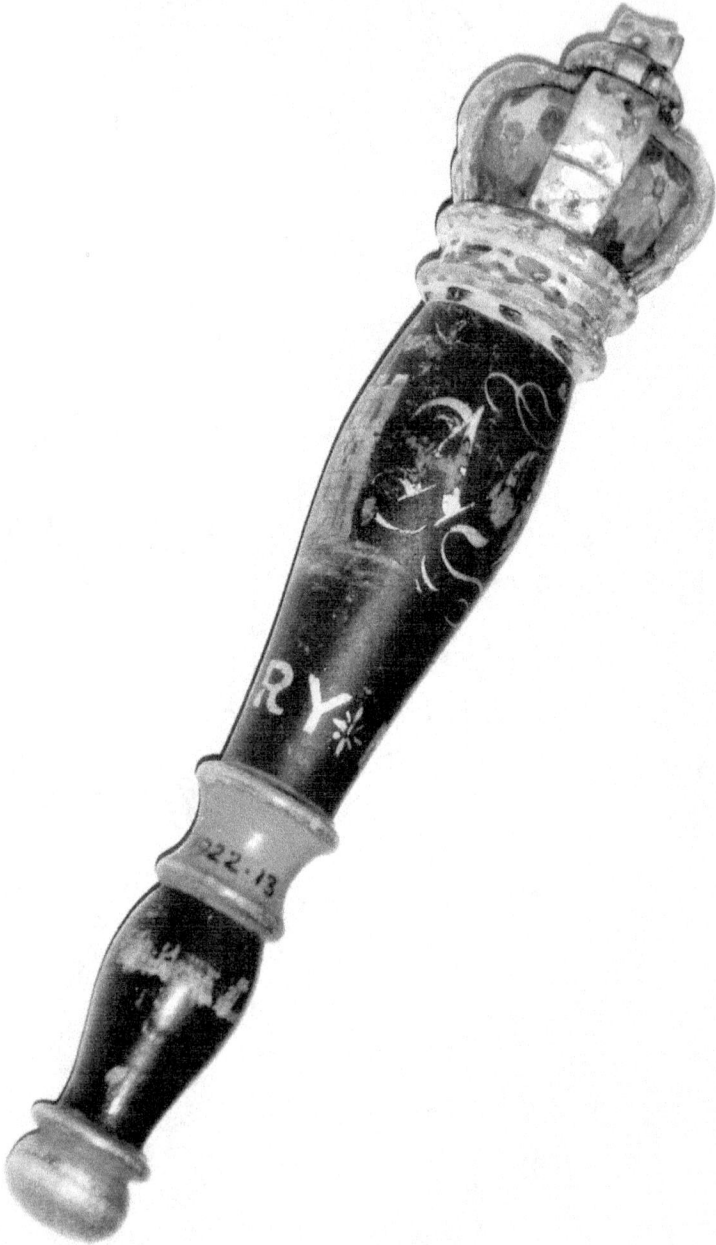

The tipstaff thought to have been issued to Alfred Milsom, the first Chief Constable

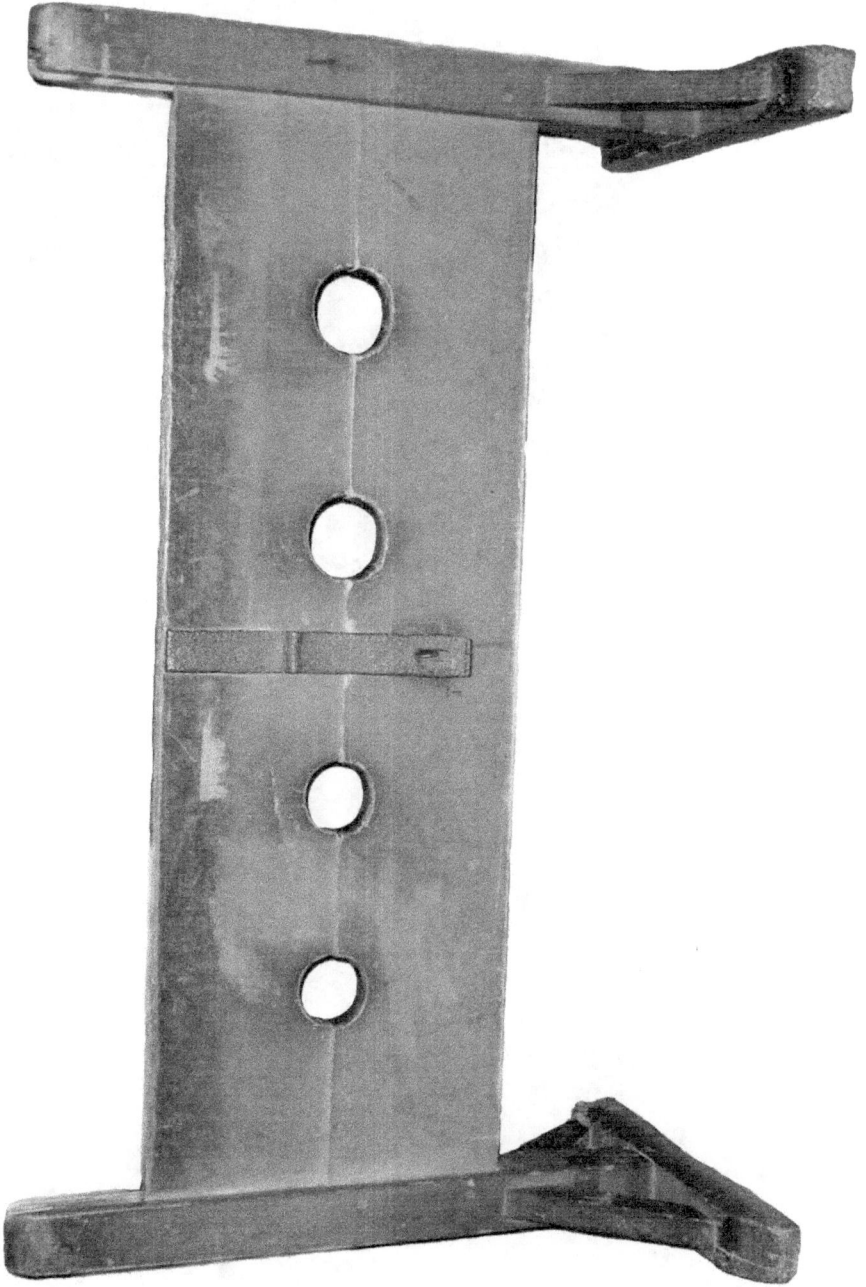

The Town Stocks

A cell door from the original Borough Jail

Early handcuffs

-*p*-

BIBLIOGRAPHY

Berkshire County Constabulary Records 1857 - 1968
(Berkshire County Record Office, Coley Avenue, Reading)
Newbury Borough Council Corporation Minute Books 1835- 1840 (N/AC1/2/1) 1840-1872.
(N/AC 1/2/2) 1873 - 1887(N/AC.l/2/3)
Numerous miscellaneous matters contained in these documents including a printed
proclamation issued by Robert Graham, Esq. relating to the enclosure ofWestfields.
(N/AP 4/33)
(Berkshire County Record Office, Coley Avenue, Reading)
Government Inspectors of Police Annual Reports 1857 - 1874
(Bramshill Police College, Hartley Witney, Hampshire)
Newbury Borough Quarter Sessions. Records and miscellaneous Court items 1836- 1871
(N/JQ I, 4 & 7)
(Berkshire County Record Office, Coley Avenue, Reading)
Newbury Borough Watch Committee Minute Book 1836 - 1845 N/AC 2/1/1
(Berkshire County Record Office, Coley Avenue, Reading)
Newbury Weekly News - Miscellaneous news items and general articles 1867 - 1875
(Newbury Central Library, The Wharf, Newbury)
Reading Mercury 1835 - 1867. Various items and general articles
(Reading Local Studies Library, Abbey Square, Reading)
The Times newspaper. Letter written by Superintendent Goddard
(The British Library [Newspaper Library] Colindale Avenue, London)
Numerous articles, items and photographs relating to the Borough of Newbury
(West Berkshire Museum, The Wharf, Newbury)

Publications

Berkshire County Constabulary, 1856 - 1956. One Hundred Years
(The Berkshire County Constabulary, W. lndge, 1956)
Berkshire to Botany Bay - A history of the 'Swing Riots ' of 1830 in Berkshire
Norman Fox
Captain Swing - A history of the Swing Riots on a national scale
Eric Hobsbawm and George Rude
The History of Her Majesty 's Inspectorate of Constabulary, The First 150 Years, 1856-2006
Home Office publication
The New Police in Nineteenth Century England, Crime Conflict and Control
David Taylor

INDEX

Aberdeen, Mr. 28
Abingdon Jail 30
Abingdon Town 4, 30, 43, 64, 69, I 04
Absalom, J (Special Constable) 124
Absalom, James (Councillor) 87, 93 , 129
Adey, Mr. (Mayor) 95, 123, 129
Adey's Barges 8
Alder, Mr. 28
Aldermaston 43
Aldridge, Robert 27-8
Alexander, John (Mayor) 9, 108, 114
Allen (Sergeant, Berkshire Police) 101-102
Allen, Charles (Constable) 70, 135
Allen, John (Joseph) (Constable) 10, 12, 16, 31, 108, 132
Andover Town 7
Andrews, Henry (Constable) 86, I 00-1 , 135
Annual Dinner 70
Army 2-3, 41, 54, 83-4, 87
Ashbury 64
Assizes, Reading 30, 35, 65-6
Association to Promote the Observance of the Liquor Licensing Law 71-72
Attewell, H (Special Constable) 124

Baby's body 23
Bailey H Special Constable 124
Bailey William (Special Constable) 124, 126
Baker, Robert (Town Clerk) I 19
Balding, W (Special Constable) 124
Barrett, Jeremiah (Constable) 83, 135
Bath (city) 7-8
Barge traffic 7-8
Bance, E J (Special Constable) 124
Banting, W (Reverend) 89, 91
Barnes, John (Berkshire Police) 43
Basing, John (Special Constable) 124
Basingstoke Town 82
Batt (Constable) 89-90, 135
Beck, Henry (Constable) 10, 12, 14, 30, 32, 40, 82, 106-8, 110, 130, 132
Becken, Mr 28
Beggars 9-1 0, I 06, 108
Beckh uson, Mr (Sheriff's Deputy) 37
Beehive Beer House 59
Bell man 10-1 2,20-1,46, 51, 82, I 06, I I 0, 130-1
Ben nett (Superintendent Berkshire County Police) 102,
Berkshire County Assizes 30, 35,65-6, 79
Berkshire County 3-6, 64, 66, 80
Berkshire County Constabulary 5-6, 40, 43, 4 7-8, 51, 55, 58, 63-4, 94, 96, 100, 103-4, 128
Berkshire Rifles 62
Bermondsey 47

Blackboys Public House 123
Blandy Colonel (Chief Constable Berkshire Police) 51, 53, 58, 96-7, 100-1
Biddis, S (Special Constable) 124
Binny, Hibbert Dr. (Rector) 25, 28-9, 31
Board of Governors 50, 75
Boshier, James (Constable) 134
Bow Street Runners I
Boxford 44
Boyer, George (Special Constable) 124
Bradfield (Constable) 134
Bradfield, James 86
Bradford 8
Bradley, Frederick 39
Bradley, Henry 34
Bradley, H (Special Constable) 126
Brazier, Thomas (Constable) 134
Brett, James 55-6
Brewers 72-3, 92
Brimpton 64
Brindley, William 79
Brooks, ET (Special Constable) 124
Brown, George (Special Constable) 127
Brown, R (Special Constable) 126
Bristol City 2, 7-8
British Army 2-3, 41
Brinen, J (Special Constable) 124
Buckeridge, William (Constable) 39, 58, 70, 76, 82, 90, 133
Buckinghamshire 4, 5
Bull, John 47
Bunny (Councillor) 9
Bunny, J (Coroner) 23
Burgess, John (Special Constable) 124
Burgess, W (Special Constable) 124
Burns, A (Special Constable) 124

Callis, G (Special Constable) 124
Canal Company 8
Carter, James (Special Constable) 127
Cattle Plague 54
Cave (Militia Sergeant) 62
Cave, W H (Mayor) 59,62, 129
Chaddleworth 44
Chall is, Cornelius (Special Constable) 126-7
Chapel - Bucklebury 44
Chieveley Village 44
Chimney Sweeps (Climbing Boys) 24
Cholsey Village I 04
Christmas Boxes 58
Christy Minstrels, The 130
Church Choir (Drum & Fife Band) 95
Church, Mr. (Commissioner) I 05
Church, William (Constable) 83, 135
City Area (Newbury) 27, 54, 59, 66, 123
City of London Police 22
Coach travellers 7

Coal Club 130

Colley, Smith & Co (Solicitors) 30

Collins, Mr. (Licensee) 89

Comyne, F (Special Constable) !24

Connell (Sergeant Militia) 84

Cook, Henry 19

Cook, W (Special Constable) 124

Cooper, John (Special Constable) 124

Copas, James (Special Constable) 124

Corn Market 6

Coroner's Inquest 2!

County & Borough Police Act, 1856 5, 41-2, 44

Creese, Henry Albert 76-7

Crimea War 41

Cromwell, Oliver 46

Crookham 44

Crosswell, George (Special Constable) 124

Crown Inn, West Mills 56

Cubbage, R (Special Constable) 124

Cullen, H (Special Constable) 124

Cunning Woman of Newbury 65-7

Davis, Thomas (Special Constable) !27

Dean, G Jnr. (Special Constable) 124

Deane, Charles (Constable) 51 , 133

Deane, George (Superintendent) 24, 30, 35, 40, 42,44-5, 48-50, 52, 57-60, 62-3, 67-7 1, 78-80, 83, 119, 127,132

Deane, Mrs 45

Dell, George 30

Dell, Thomas 30

Dellor, Mr. 88

Dell or, T (Special Constable) 124

Derby 2

Devizes 8, 69

Dibley (Constable) 51, 134

Dinner (Annual) 70

Disturbances 26-9

Dog Carts 32-3

Dog Rapper 12

Dolton (Councillor) 98-9

Dore, Benjamin (Special Constable) 124, 127

Dore, W (Special Constable) !24

Dorl, Lewis 46, 48

Dowde, George (Supt. Berkshire Constabulary) 43

Dowdeswell, G M (Q.C.) 76

Dredge, David 48

Dredge, William (Mayor I Councillor) 9, 37-9, 119-20

Dyne, Mr. (Builder) 36-7

Eagle Public House 55, 76, 89-90

East Ilsley 43-4

Eastbury I 04

Eastfields Enclosure 26, 31

Election Disturbances 36-8, 53, 68, 126

Elkins, Samuel (Constable) 132

Fairs 23, 31 , 33, 68, 92, 126-8

Faringdon 43, 64

Female shoplifters 23

Fenians 61, 123, 126

Fidler, Thomas 45, 73, 85, 93-4

Finch, CD (Special Constable) 124

Fire Brigade 49-50, 57-8, 69, 83, 126-7

Fisher, Mr. 76,79

Flint, John (Councillor) 9, 87, 107

Flint, S (Special Constable) 124

Flint's Barges 8

Fly Boats 8

Fox, John (Special Constable) 124

Fraser (Chief Constable Berkshire) 43

Freeman, S H (Special Constable) 124

Frewin, Esther (Matron - Jail) 26, 45, 126

Frewin, James 34, 39, 40, 44, 126-7

Fullbrook, William (Constable) 58, 82-4, 87, 100-3, 127, 134

Gammon, Thomas (Special Constable) 126

Gatehouse, William (Constable) 21,132

Gauntlett, Hugh (Constable) 35, 134

Gayzer, H (Special Constable) 124

Gibbs, Charles (Special Constable) 127

Gibbs, William (Special Constable) 127

Giles, Maria 66

Gilmore, Mrs. 88, 91

Goddard, George (Superintendent) 64, 74-9, 83-102, 125, 135

Goddard, Richard 74-5, 86-8, 93

Goddard, Mrs. 88

Goodchild, John (Constable) 82-3, 135

Gordon Riots 2

Gosling, Caleb (Special Constable) 127

Goulter, Mr. (Solicitor) 78

Government Inspector 44-8, 57, 64-5, 81 ,84

Graham, Mr. R F 27

Graham, T W (Special Constable) 124

Gray, Edward Will iam (Councillor) 9-1 0, !9-20, 107, I I 1-2, I 16, 118

Gray, M (Special Constable) 124

Green, Mr. 23

Green, Mrs. 23

Greenham (Parish) 6, 47

Grey, Sir George (Home Secretary) 32

Griffin, W (Special Constable) 124

Griffiths, Caleb (Constable) 70, I 27, 135

Griffiths, W (Special Constable) I 24

Gun Public House 79

Hall, Alfred (Special Constable) 127

Hampstead Norreys 44, 66

Hand & Heart Public House 55

Handley, John (Sergeant) 60, 64, 135

Harfield, William (Supt. Berkshire Police) 43, 55-6, 63

Harrison, E (Special Constable) 124
Hawk, Captain 65
Hayes, G (Sergeant Fi re Brigade) 57, 127
Hayward, Mr. 88
Hickman, J (Mayor) 40, 87, 94
Hickman, W (Special Constable) 124
Higgs, E (Special Constable) 124
Hill, John (Sergeant) 35, 46, 49, 133
Hinds, Thomas (Sergeant) 48, 5 1, 55, 59-60, 133
Hiring Fairs 3 1, 33
Hobbs, Joseph (Tythingman) 126
Hockley, Henry (Special Constable) 127
Home Secretary 14, 19, 20-1 , 25, 32-3, 40, 44,
52, 6 1,
71,85, 103, 113, 120-1
Horse Dealers 26
Hungerford 30, 36, 39, 43, 62
Hungerford Magistrates Court 62

Industrial Revolution 2
lnkpen 44, 62
Ireland 61

Jackson (Alderman) 92
Jackson, W H (Special Constable) 124
Jail (Newbury) 5, 15, 17, 22, 26, 34, 48, 58, 69, 83,
88, 115
Jail break 17
James, M (Councillor) 9, I 07
Jarrett, G (Special Constable) 124
Joblen, W (Tythingman) 126
Jones, Alfred 87
Justice, Stephen (Constable) 45 , 5 1, 58, 60, 83,
134
Justices of the Peace I, 3, 5, 37-9, 42, 49, 60-1, 63,
72, 82

Kimber, John (Councillor) 9-1 0, 19, 107, 1ll, 116
Kimber, Thomas (Constable) 50, 134
King, David (Constable) 10, 12, 16, 108, 132
King, J (Constable) 31, 132
King, T G (Special Constable - Supt.) 124
King, W. W (Special Constable - Sergeant) 124
Kintbury 44, 102
Knight, W (Special Constable) 124
Knight, William (Special Constable) 126-7

Lack, E (Special Constable) 124
Lamb Public House 123
Lambourn 42
Langton, J (Special Constable) 124
Langton, Thomas (Constable) 35, 134
Langton, William (Night Constable) 10, 12, 16-7,
19, 22-4, 34, 108, 1ll , 11 6, 11 8, 132-3
Langton, William Jnr. (Constable) 34, 133
Lee, John 46-7
Letter to The Times newspaper 85, 90-4, 125

Lewis, Benny (Constable) 52, 133
Licensing Act 1872 74, 85 , 88, 125
Liddiard, George (Special Constable) 124
Liddiard, Janles (Constable) 133
Liddiard, James (Special Constable) 124
Lighting & Watching Act 1833 4
Liverpool 72
Lloyd, George 11
London I, 3, 7-8, 40- 1, 47, 55, 66, 104
London Apprentice Public House 123
Long, Thomas (Tythingman) 126
Long Wittenham 104
Looker, S H (Special Constable) 124
Lucas, C (Special Constable) 124
Lucas, Charles (Solicitor) 9 1-3, 99-1 00

Maidenhead 4, 82
Marlborough 82
Marr, C W (Special Constable) 124
Martin, Henry 55 -7
Martin, Joseph 79
Martin, Mr. (Councillor) 38
Martin, R (Special Constable) 124
Match Women & Boys 9, 106
Matthews, H J (Special Constable) 124
Mayo, G (Special Constable) 124
Meakins, H (Special Constable) 124
Metropolitan Police 3, 47-8, 64, 68, 76, 104
Metropolitan Police Act 1829 3, 22
Michaelmas Fair 33, 68, 94, 126-7,
Millers Public House 76
Milsom, Alfred (Chief Constable) I 0-1 2,
20, 22, 28, 30, 33, 35, 106-8, 11 6-7, 11 9, 132
Money, Waiter 91
Morris, William (Special Constable) 126
Municipal Corporations Act 1835 4, 5, 9-1 0, 40,
105, 109, 111

Nags Head Public House 69
Napoleonic Wars 2, 41
Navvies 8, 103
New Inn Public House 74, 86, 88
Newbery, Henry Thomas (Special Constable) 126
Newbury Association for the Apprehension of
Thieves & Felons 1
Newbury Borough I, 3-6, 8-9, I 0-11 , 13, 15, 20,
32, 44, 67, 72, 84, 96, 102, 105, 108-9, 128 -
Newbury Brass Band 95
Newbury Herald 120
Newbury Highwayman 65-6
Newbury Temperance Society 7 1-2, 85, 91
Newbury Weekly News 59, 66, 72-5, 78, 86-7, 90,
93-5, 97, 99-1 02, 124
Newton, Thomas (Special Constable - Sergeant)
124
Neyler, Robert (Coachman) 23
Night Watch System (Newbury) 4, 9, 11, 14,

North, Thomas (Special Constable) 127
North, William (Constable) 34, 133
North, William (Landlord) 59
North, William (Special Constable) 127
Nottingham 2
November 5th celebrations 33
Noyes, George (Constable) 33, 39, 133

Newton, Thomas (Special Constable - Sergeant) 124
Neyler, Robert (Coachman) 23
Night Watch System (Newbury) 4, 9, 11, 14,
North, Thomas (Special Constable) 127
North, William (Constable) 34, 133
North, William (Landlord) 59
North, William (Special Constable) 127
Nottingham 2
November 5th celebrations 33
Noyes, George (Constable) 33, 39, 133

O'Brien, W (Special Constable) 124
Optimus Coach Company 23
Oxford 4, 5, 7, 102
Oxford City Police 5
Oxfordshire County Constabulary 4

Packer, J (Special Constable) 124
Palmer, Robert (MP) 41
Palmerston, Lord 40-1
Panting, R (Special Constable) 124
Paris, Charles (Special Constable) 124
Parish Constables 1, 5, 15, 69,114
Parliamentary Reform 3
Paulin, George (Constable) 51, 133
Pauling, (Paulding) George (Special Constable) 127
Payne, George (Councillor) 9-1 0, 19, 111 , 116
Payne, T (Special Constable) 127
Pearce, Alfred (Special Constable) 127
Pearce, Charles (Special Constable) 12 7
Peasemore 44
Pelican Inn 7, 44
Pelican Lane, County Police Station 44, 65
Pennington, W J (Special Constable) 124
Penrice, James (Special Constable) 127
Pension Scheme 50
Perry, Charles (Constable) 60, 135
Perry, Charles Richard (Special Constable) 127
Perry, Jonathan 17
Philpot, J (Special Constable) 124
Piercey, Mr. 28
Pigeons Beer House 20
Pinniger, J C (Special Constable) 124
Pitman, William (Special Constable) 127
Ploughman, Mr. 69
Plummer, E (Special Constable) 124
Polehill, E (Special Constable) 124
Police Gazette 25, 29

Police Managers 11, 19, 109, 11 6
Polling disturbances 36-8, 68
Poole, G (Special Constable) 124
Pratt (Councillor) 87,93, 129
Presentment to Quarter Sessions 72-3
Price, Thomas (Yeoman of Speen) 30
Profane Material 32
Purdue, H (Special Constable) 124
Purdue, Thomas (Special Constable) 127
Purdue, William (Highwayman) 65
Purton, John (Special Constable) 127

Quarter Sessions 5, 11 , 17, 2 1, 30, 42, 46,72-3, 76, 79

Rabies 42
Railway Navvies 8, 103
Railways 8, 34
Reading Borough Police 4-5, 24-5, 43, 60, 69, 82
Reading Mercury 36, 120
Reading Prison 46, 55, 60, 82
Reading, Henry 4 7
Regiment of Foot (76th) 67
Relieving Officer 69, 83
Riot Act 36, 38
Rivers, Isaac 66
Roake, J J (Special Constable) 124
Robinson, E (Special Constable) 124
Robinson, R (Surgeon) 23
Rose, John William (Sergeant) 47-8, 64, 133
Rosier, Thomas (Constable) 52, 58, 70, 134
Royal Exchange Insurance Company 57
Royal Humane Society 80
Runaway husbands 24
Russell, Lord (Home Secretary) 14,20, 113
Ryott, R A (Mayor) 73, 77, 78

Salisbury 7
Salway, E (Special Constable) 124
Samuels (Constable) 134
Samuels (Jailer) 17, 34
Samuels, William (Special Constable) 127
Sangwell, C (Special Constable) 124
Sargent, B (Special Constable) 124
Satchell, John (Alderman) 9, 107
Saunders, C (Special Constable) 124
Savory, James (Constable) 133
Scard, H B (Special Constable) 124
Second World War 4 1, 49
Self Self (Recorder) 119
Shaw, Eliza 55-7
Shaw, John (Councillor) 9-10, 19, 38, Ill , 11 6, 123
Shaw, John Richard (Sergeant) 64, 135
Shaw (Parish) 6, 55
Shefford 44
Shinfield (Parish) 24
Sindle, Alfred 65-6
Slade, J Jnr. (Special Constable) 124

Slade, John (Tythingman) 126
Slocock, Edmund (Alderman) 9, 107
Smallpox 30
Smith, Harry 69
Smith, Henry James (Special Constable) 124
Smith, Jane 30
Smith, R (Special Constable) 124
Smith's Coffee Shop 123
Southampton 40
Special Assizes 3
Special Constables 2-3, 27, 3 1, 3 7-8, 49, 53, 61
62-3, 68, 70, 94, 126, 128
Speen 6, 23
Speenhamland 6-7, 23, 36, 97, 128
Staples, John (Tythingman) 126
Stillman, Frederick (Special Constable) 127
Stillman, William (Sergeant) 70, 80, 84, 86, 97-
101, 127, 135, 143
Stocks 61, 82
Stone, F (Corporal) 57, 127
Stone, F (Special Constable) 124
Stone, J B (Special Constable) 124
Stroud, William (Constable) 20-1, 132
Sulhampstead I 04
Summersby (Constable) 86, 100-1 , 135
Sumpster, W (Special Constable) 124
Sun Beer House 55
Superannuation Fund 50, 52. 60, 84, 99, I 00
Sutton Courtney I 04
Swan, W (Special Constable) 124
Swindon 8
Swing Riots 2-3, 12, 103

Taylor (Constable) 94, 135
Taylor (Fireman I Engineer) 57, 127
Taylor, Henry (Special Constable) 126
Taylor, William (Special Constable) 127
Teal, William 62-3
Tegg, John (Constable) 79, 95, 100, 102, 104, 135
Temperance Society 71-2, 85, 91
Tewson (Constable) 132
Testimonial, Sergeant Goddard 78
Testimonial, Superintendent Deane 79-80
Thames Valley Police 4-5
Thatcham 44, 104
Thatcher, S (Special Constable) 124
Theatre (Newbury) 7
Thomas, F (Special Constable) 126
Thorn, George (Special Constable) 127
Three Tuns Public House 67, 86
Threshing machines 2
Times newspaper 25, 85, 90-3
Tomkins, John (Constable) 16, 19, 32, 132
Town Crier 20-1 , 46, I 06
Town Sergeant I Town Crier 20-1, 81-2
Town Wharf 8
Tranter, T (Special Constable) 124

Tranter, William 66
Trowbridge 8
Trumplett, John (Councillor) 9-10, 107, 111
Tuck, Mark 82
Turn-out (Free grazing) 26-7
Tythingmen 15, 107, 114, 126

Vardy, M W (Printer) 108
Vestries 4
Vigilance Committee 72
Vincent (Councillor) 9
Vines, Joseph (Clerk of the Peace) 119

Waddington (Home Secretary) 52-3, 121
Wait, Henry (Constable) 32, 133
Wallace, Elizabeth 67
Wallen, John (Constable) I 0, 12, 20, 1`06-8, 132
Wallingford 4, l04
Wantage 4, 43, 104
War Office 87
Ward, William 79
Warner, Thomas (Constable) 35, 134
Warwick, Constable 132
Wash Common Beat 79, 122
Watchmen I, 4, 8-9, 12,
Watts, T (Special Constable) 127
Webster, W H (Special Constable) 124
Weights & Measures 57-8 ,69, 83
West Mi ll s Wharf 8, 98
Westfields Enclosures 26-8
Weston, Benjan1in (Treasurer) 119
Weston, lsaac (Constable) 10, 12, 16, 24, 108, 132
Whately, Mr. (Recorder) 25
Wheeler, William (Special Constable) 124
White Horse Cellar (Piccadilly) 23 , 127
Whiting, John (Constable) 33, 39, 133
Wickham 44
Wilder, Edward (Constable) I 0, 12, 16, 32, 108, 132
Wilkinson, S J (Special Constable) 124
Willes, George (Captain)36, 38, 39, 120
Willis, Captain (Government Inspector) 49, 58, 96
Willis, E (Special Constable) 124
Willis, R (Special Constable) 124
Willis, T (Special Constable) 124
Winchester 7
Window Tax 34
Windsor Borough 4, 43
Windsor, E (Special Constable) 124
Windsor, Mr. 51
Winsons, Mr. 51, 123
Witchcraft 65
Witherington, Mr. (Baker) 130
Witherington, William (Tythingman) 126
Withers, J (Special Constable) 124
Wyatt, James (Constable) 32, 58, 70, 133
Wyvell (or Wyatt), Vincent (Constable) 134

York 40